Managing Editor
Mara Ellen Guckian

Illustrator
Kelly McMahon

Cover Artist
Barb Lorseyedi

Editor in Chief
Ina Massler Levin, M.A.

Creative Director
Karen J. Goldfluss, M.S. Ed.

Art Coordinator
Renée Christine Yates

Imaging
James Edward Grace
Craig Gunnell

Publisher

Mary D. Smith, M.S. Ed.

YEAR-ROUND
THEMES
GOING PLACES

INCLUDES CD-ROM OF FULL-COLOR PATTERNS!

Literacy Skills

Social Skills

Motor Skills

OCEAN · FARM · PUMPKIN PATCH · POND · WINTER WONDERLAND

Includes Standards & Benchmarks

Author

Kim Fields

Teacher Created Resources, Inc.
6421 Industry Way
Westminster, CA 92683
www.teachercreated.com
ISBN: 978-1420-6-2392-5
© 2010 Teacher Created Resources, Inc.
Made in U.S.A.

Teacher Created Resources

Table of Contents

Table of Contents (cont.)

Let's Go to the Pond!

Off We Go!

Let's Go to the Ocean!

Off We Go!

Passport

Introduction

Year-Round Themes: Going Places has all you need to get started with a thematic approach for a year full of adventures, including a color CD to produce ready-to-use puppets and props. Teaching thematically is one of the preferred methods of preschool instruction for the following reasons:

- Children are provided with meaningful repetition of content over a period of time. The repetition of a theme during the day, week, or month brings security and familiarity to preschool children. They thrive when routines and predictable activities are used consistently.

- Children are able to recall and apply key vocabulary and concepts that help build connections between the theme, themselves, and their world.

- Children are given multiple opportunities to practice readiness skills such as recognizing rhyming sounds, oral fluency, and listening comprehension.

- Children can communicate more easily about a particular subject because teaching thematically provides an enriched language environment. Children learn differently. Providing vocabulary benefits all types of learning styles and special needs.

- Depending on the children's interests and needs, themes can be expanded or extended.

Preschoolers are always on the go and *Year-Round Themes: Going Places* takes your children exactly where they want to go—on "trips" packed with engaging learning! This book includes the following itinerary for each unit destination:

- **Off We Go!** provides suggestions to introduce the travel plan which will be your theme.

- **Ready, Set, Rhyme!** sets the tone for the exploration. A related Rhyming Story based on a familiar tale, complete with presentation ideas, extends the literacy concepts addressed.

- **Cross-Curricular Excursions** provide small-group activities and learning center ideas for each new location.

- **On the Move** offers movement activities and music ideas to celebrate the journey.

- **Souvenir Sharing** provides a culminating school-home connection project and letter to parents to share the travel experience.

A passport is included in the last section of this book so that each child can track his or her journey to each destination. When travel to one of the five destinations has been completed, a sticker or stamp may be added to the page, and a finish date may be stamped. (See page 205 for directions to complete the passport.)

By utilizing *Year-Round Themes: Going Places* with your curious and adventurous young learners, you can be confident that you are providing them with a solid knowledge base that will be added to throughout their lives. Share action-packed adventures with your preschoolers to a variety of delightful destinations—even if you never leave the school site. Your young travelers are certain to improve their vocabulary and gain a multitude of important readiness skills along the way. There's so much to see and do!

How to Use This Book

Each section of *Year-Round Themes: Going Places*, from background information to culmination, is fun and motivating. The full-color CD allows the teacher to create color props and puppets for each unit in a snap. Additional information and pictures can be found online. Age-appropriate standards and benchmarks are provided for each activity. The units are Head Start themes, as well.

The five sections described below for each unit will help you plan your adventures to a farm, a pumpkin patch, a winter wonderland, a pond, and the ocean. Get those passports made. (See page 205.) What are you waiting for? It's time to get going!

Off We Go!

Off We Go! is the introductory section for each unit. This section provides ideas and materials to build excitement for the trip (theme). Adorable patterns provide visual support for young learners. Color versions of the patterns from the CD may be prepared for classroom use to spark further interest. Additional copies can be made for student use, or children can color their own versions using the corresponding black-and-white reproducibles in the book. Coloring and manipulating puppets are excellent ways to practice fine-motor development. You will find additional ways to use them and directions for the storage and display of props on page 7 and in individual units.

Also included in this section is a list of related, hands-on materials to help introduce the theme to the children. Questions about the destination draw on the children's prior experience with the topic and raise awareness of the concepts they would like to explore in the future.

You will find a Suggested Books list to further enhance your visit to each new location. These books, and others in your library, may be incorporated in a variety of ways, from introducing the children to new information to reinforcing or reviewing previously learned concepts. You may also wish to check online for appropriate virtual field trips, pictures, photographs, and videos.

An extensive list of related vocabulary has also been compiled for each destination. Incorporate these words into daily language whenever possible; encourage the children to do likewise. Review the vocabulary words on a regular basis.

Ready, Set, Rhyme!

A wonderful thematic rhyming story is incorporated into each unit. For example, you may integrate "The Three Little Pigs" Rhyming Story (See pages 18–26.) into your exploration of the farm. Ideas for presenting each rhyming story are provided. Patterns to use during the presentation of the rhyming story are provided in black-and-white, and also in color on the CD. Copy these patterns onto heavy cardstock to use for group activities.

After your children are familiar with the unit's rhyming story, use the Revisiting the Rhyming Story ideas in the unit to reinforce readiness skills. Participating in developmentally appropriate readiness activities can be the key to a successful reading experience in later years. The rhyming stories in each thematic unit in this book contain repetitive rhymes, rhythms, and phrases that will stimulate interest and engage student participation.

A list of Readiness Standards addressed by the activities is provided in each Ready, Set, Rhyme! section. Many standards relate to reading readiness. Others address motor skill development.

How to Use This Book (cont.)

Ready, Set, Rhyme! (cont.)

The following are a sample of readiness standards included in this book:

- recognizes rhyming sounds
- retells stories using picture cues
- comprehends text read aloud by the teacher
- participates in CLOZE activities (repetitive phrases)
- develops oral fluency (smooth, easy reading/speaking)
- understands left-to-right directionality
- follows two- to three-step directions
- uses and understands appropriate vocabulary

Finally, discuss with the children the Character Concept idea for each story. Discuss the qualities suggested and how children might implement them into their daily lives.

Cross-Curricular Excursions

No preschool thematic unit would be complete without learning centers! A variety of different activities for your writing, math, block, art, and cooperative learning centers are included in *Year-Round Themes: Going Places*. These activities can be used to add pair and small group work to your program. Participating in the learning center activities will help children develop necessary math, cognitive, writing, oral language, fine motor, and social skills now and help them meet important standards later.

On the Move

Providing preschoolers with opportunities for active learning acknowledges their need to move and express themselves physically. Physical activity not only keeps children engaged but it also maximizes learning and makes it fun. Suggestions for theme-related, gross-motor activities have been included for each unit to get your children learning on the move. They will imitate a variety of movements and sounds, follow directions, take turns, and cooperate with others.

Souvenir Sharing

Round out each unit with a special school-home connection project. For instance, after your visit to the farm, have your children create the Souvenir Barn Baskets (see pages 38–43). The culminating activity for each unit will serve as a prompt to review what the children have learned about the location "visited." More importantly, it provides each child with a souvenir to take home and share what he or she has learned.

These souvenir projects can take a few days to complete, but they are a wonderful way to end a unit and are certain to generate discussion at school and at home. These activities tend to need a bit of extra adult help, either in the preparation phase or during assembly. These would be great days to have extra parent helpers.

For each Souvenir Sharing activity, make a copy of the School-Home Connection Ticket for each child. Send the copy home, along with the handmade souvenir, encouraging children to share what they have learned with their families. Parents can use the prompts on the School-Home Connection Ticket as a springboard for discussions, songs, stories, and other activities from their "journey."

Puppets and Props

Using the Stick Puppets

Stick puppets should be used by teachers and children alike to retell rhymes, songs, and stories. Children should also be encouraged to create new stories using puppets from the different stories. For added interest, create a puppet theater or a special area in the room where students can put on shows using the puppets and other props.

How to Make Stick Puppets

Use the CD to print out color versions of the patterns in the book. Cut the patterns out, and attach them to craft sticks or straws. If possible, print on one-sided glossy paper to avoid needing to laminate! If glossy paper is not available, lamination is suggested to create longer-lasting props. Black-and-white versions can also be colored, cut out, and then added to craft sticks. Children often enjoy personalizing their puppets and props. The more they can participate in the process of creating the story components, the more opportunities they will have to develop the fine motor skills necessary to color, cut, and paste.

Stick-Puppet Displays and Storage Containers

Simple puppet displays can be made using shoeboxes or other boxes with lids. Decorate each box and label it with the name of the unit. Cut small slits in the top of the box lid for each pattern and slide the stick puppets in. (See example below.)

Copies of the unit story and the puppets can be stored in the box when not in use. To help keep track of different sets, list the contents of each box on the inside of the box lid. Create a set of storage boxes to be used again and again. If possible, store them where they will be accessible to children.

Let's Go to the Farm!

Materials
- Farm Animal Patterns on pages 11–15 or the color versions, farm animals.pdf, on the CD
- Farm Scene on pages 16–17 or the color version, farm scene.pdf, on the CD
- farm-related items (e.g., fresh fruit, straw hat, plastic farm animals)
- tray
- tag board or foam core

Teacher Preparation
1. Copy and color a class set of Farm Animal Patterns, or make color copies, and cut them out.
2. Collect a variety of farm-related items (e.g., fresh fruit and vegetables, eggs, a straw hat, a plastic farm animal) and display them on a tray.
3. Combine pages 16 and 17 to create the farm scene. Mount it on tag board or foam core.

Procedure
1. Have the children sit together in a group during circle or whole-group time. It is important for all children to be able to see the visual aids and hear the responses from classmates.
2. Introduce the unit by presenting the selected visuals, simple questions, and facts about the farm.

Where are we going?

Explain to the children that, in their classroom, they will be learning about farms. They will be reading about farm life, examining farm products, and learning even more about farm animals. They will learn many new things that will help them imagine they are part of a real farm!

Read a farm-themed book to the children. Use a classroom favorite or choose a new one from the Suggested Books listed on page 9. Show the children a collection of farm-related items in a basket. Ask them where they think these things are found. Then explain to the children that they will be studying farms. Ask them what they know about farms. *A farm is an area of land where animals (livestock) and/or crops are raised.* Invite the children who have visited a farm to briefly describe their experiences. Share the Farm Scene with children and point out the different areas. Ask, "Which animal might live here?"

Who/what will we see at the farm?

Ask children who or what they might see at a farm. *They might see animals, a barn, a house, a tractor, different kinds of crops, and farmers and other workers.* Remind children that, besides animals, a farm must also have people to take care of the animals and the crops. Prepare the Farm Animal Patterns for display on a flannel or magnetic board. Discuss the display. Help children brainstorm other things they might see on a farm. You might wish to start a chart with pictures and labels. Encourage children to add to the chart for the duration of the journey to the farm. Incorporate the words from the Farm Vocabulary list on page  10 whenever possible. Review the vocabulary words daily with the children.

Let's Go to the Farm! *(cont.)*

Procedure *(cont.)*

What could we do at the farm?

Review the five senses. Ask children about how they might use each sense when observing a farm. They might *see* a farmer on a tractor, *hear* cows mooing, *taste* apples picked from a tree, *touch* horses, and *smell* freshly cut hay.

When is the best time to visit the farm?

Ask children when they would visit a farm. *A good time to visit a farm to see harvesting would be in the fall. A good time to see baby animals might be in the spring.*

What type of clothes would you wear?

Ask children what they should wear on the visit to the farm. *A farm is outdoors. You might choose to wear play clothes, such as blue jeans, and sturdy boots or shoes in case you have to walk through mud! Wearing a hat to provide shade from the sun would also be a good idea.*

Why would you like to visit the farm?

Invite children to give reasons why they would like to visit a farm. *You could see animals, farm vehicles and equipment, and find out where some of our food grows!*

Suggested Books

A Chick Hatches by Joanna Cole

Barn Cat by Carol P. Saul

Barnyard Banter by Denise Fleming

Big Red Barn by Margaret Wise Brown

Daisy and the Beastie by Jane Simmons

Farm Counting Book by Jane Miller

I Went Walking by Sue Williams

Old MacDonald Had a Farm by Jane Cabrera

Over on the Farm: A Counting Picture Book Rhyme by Christopher Gunson

Snappy Little Farmyard by Dugald Steer

Farm Vocabulary

People
farmer
trainer
veterinarian
workers

Vehicles & Machines
combine
hayrack
milking machine
pickup truck
planter
tractor

Areas
field
garden
hayloft
meadow
orchard
pasture
trough

Farm Products
berries
eggs
feathers
fruits
fur
grains
leather
milk
nuts
seeds
vegetables
wool

Buildings
barn
coop
doghouse
farmhouse
hutch
pen
silo
stable
stall

Tools
basket
hoe
pail
pitchfork
plow
rope
shovel
wheelbarrow

Animal Foods
grains   grass   hay   insects   worms

Animal	Baby	Mother	Father
cow	calf	cow	bull
goat	kid	nanny	billy
horse	foal (filly/colt)	mare	stallion
pig	piglet	sow	boar
rabbit	kit	doe	buck
sheep	lamb	ewe	ram
chicken	chick	hen	rooster
duck	duckling	duck	drake
goose	gosling	goose	gander
turkey	poult	hen	tom

Farm Animal Patterns

Baby Mammals

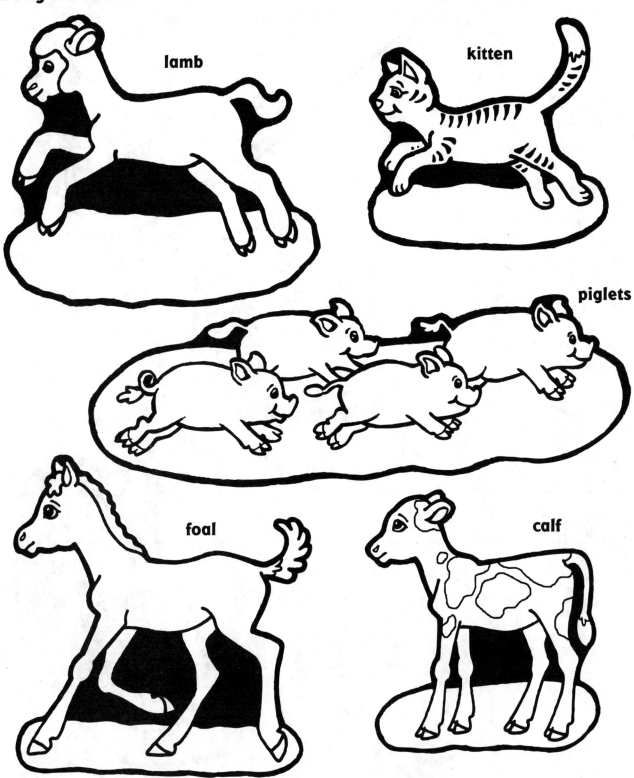

Note: Once children are familiar with each farm animal's name, the patterns can be used for sorting activities—birds/mammals; 2 legs/4 legs.

Farm Animal Patterns *(cont.)*

Birds

duck

chicks

hen

goose

turkey

rooster

ducklings

Note: Once children are familiar with each farm animal's name, the patterns can be used for sorting activities—birds/mammals; 2 legs/4 legs.

Farm Animal Patterns *(cont.)*

Mammals

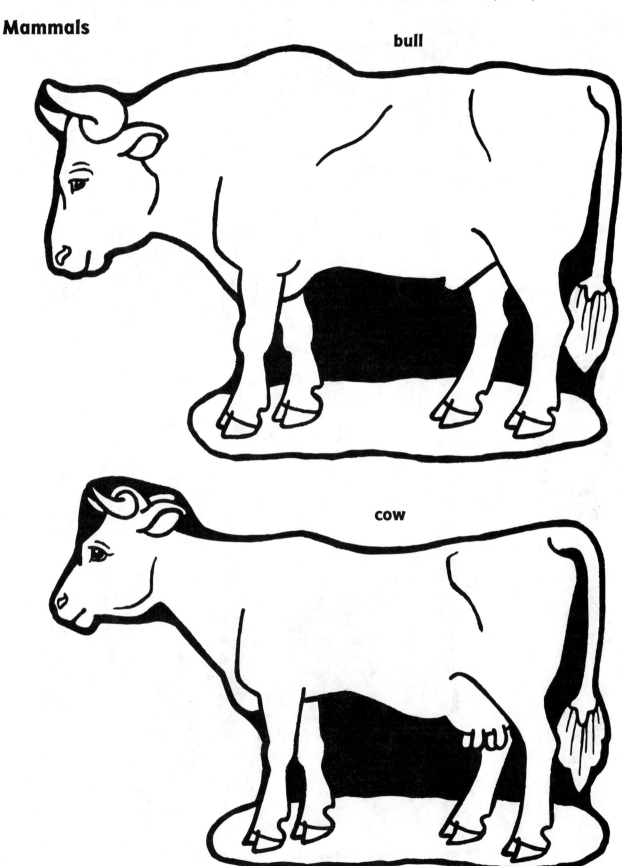

bull

cow

Farm Animal Patterns *(cont.)*

Mammals

sheep

horse

Farm Animal Patterns *(cont.)*

Mammals

pig

dog

goat

rabbit

Farm Scene

Farm Scene *(cont.)*

"The Three Little Pigs"

Readiness Standards

Reading

- understands left-to-right directionality
- recognizes rhyming sounds
- uses pictures to retell stories
- understands that illustrations should convey meaning

Materials

- "The Three Little Pigs" rhyming story poster on pages 20–21 or the color version, three pigs story.pdf, on the CD
- "The Three Little Pigs" Patterns on pages 22–26 or the color versions, three pigs patterns.pdf, on the CD
- Velcro® (adhesive hook and loop)
- sheet of poster board
- markers

Teacher Preparation

1. Color, cut out, and laminate the story and patterns. Attach the hook side of the Velcro® to the back of each character, house, and wheelbarrow.

2. Prepare a storyboard on a sheet of poster board as shown below. Draw a simple road along the bottom of the poster.

3. Attach the loop side of the Velcro where the characters and houses will be placed. The characters and houses should be placed sequentially from left to right to tell the story.

4. Plan to spend a few days immersing students in the rhyming version of "The Three Little Pigs" story. The more you read the story to the children, the more familiar they will become with it and the more they will be able to participate.

   - **Preview** new vocabulary, such as *jig*, *sturdy*, *abode*, *slinks*, and *scurries*.
   - **Discuss/Practice** the refrains: "Let me come in!" "Not by the hair of my chinny-chin-chin!" "I'm the toughest wolf in town! I'll huff and puff and blow your house down!"

5. Story presentation suggestions are provided on the following page in the Procedure section.

"The Three Little Pigs" *(cont.)*

Procedure

1. Explain to the children that you will be sharing a version, of "The Three Little Pigs" that rhymes. Introduce the main characters: Baby Pig, Sister Pig, and Brother Pig.

2. Hand out the story patterns. Explain to the children that some of them will add patterns to the board and others will have turns moving or removing the patterns as the story unfolds.

3. Read "The Three Little Pigs" rhyming story to the group. Instruct a child to attach a character, wheelbarrow, or house when it is mentioned.

4. Have a child remove a house when it is blown away and move the appropriate pig to the next house. (At the end of the story, all three pigs should be at the brick house.)

Revisiting the Rhyming Story

Once children are familiar with the rhyming version of "The Three Little Pigs," try the following activities:

1. Substitute other farm animals for the characters of the wolf and the pig. Which farm animal might make a faster runner than a pig in this story? (*goat, horse*) Instead of the wolf, which farm animal might chase other animals in this story? (*dog, rooster*) Tell the story using the new suggestions.

2. Have the children use the patterns and the storyboard to retell the story of "The Three Little Pigs." (See the illustration on page 18.)

3. Focus on the rhyming words in the story. Ask each child to hold a Wolf puppet. Explain that you will be reading pairs of words to them and that you want them to have their wolves "blow" if the pair of words you read rhymes. If the pair of words does not rhyme, ask them to have the wolf say, "Not by the hair of my chinny-chin-chin!"

For example:

Road and *abode* are a rhyming pair, so the children would make the wolf blow.

Brother and *sister* are not rhyming words, so the children would have the wolf say, "Not by the hair of my chinny, chin, chin!"

Rhyming Word Pairs		Non-rhyming Word Pairs	
drive—five	play—day	brother—sister	neatest—toughest
huffs—puffs	stay—away	builds—blows	street—straw
house—mouse	sticks—bricks	dance—down	sturdy—strong
in—chin	sticks—tricks	hair—house	walks—runs
might—kite	straw—saw	he—his	wolf—pig
might—sight	street—treat	mad—might	work—play
pig—jig	town—down		

Character Concept

The Wolf in the story actually had a good character trait: *determination.* He continued to huff and puff, even if he did not catch the pigs! He kept trying and trying.

- Ask the children how the pigs showed determination. *They kept running away from the wolf and going to the next house.*

- Ask the children to think of times when they have shown determination.

"The Three Little Pigs"

Three little pigs have no time to play.
They each build a house, they work all day!
Baby Pig builds a house with straw,
The neatest straw house you ever saw!
Sister Pig builds a house with sturdy sticks,
Brother Pig builds a house with strong bricks.

Here comes Wolf, sneaking down the road.
He walks right up to the straw abode.
"Baby Pig, Baby Pig, let me come in!"
"Not by the hair of my chinny-chin-chin!"
"I'm the toughest wolf in town!
I'll huff and puff and blow your house down!"

Wolf huffs and puffs with all his might,
Baby Pig's straw house blows out of sight.
Baby Pig runs to the house of Sister Pig,
Just in time to dance a little jig!
Wolf slinks on down the street,
While dreaming of a tasty treat.

Wolf sees two pigs in a house of sticks,
The hungry Wolf is up to his old tricks.
"Sister Pig, Sister Pig, let me come in!"
"Not by the hair of my chinny-chin-chin!"
"I'm the toughest wolf in town!
I'll huff and puff and blow your house down!"

Wolf huffs and puffs with all his might,
Sister Pig's stick house blows away like a kite.
Baby Pig and Sister Pig race away,
They run to Brother Pig's house to stay.
Wolf scurries on down the drive,
He's getting mad; he should count to five!

Wolf sees three pigs in a brick house,
So he tiptoes to the door as quick as a mouse.
"Brother Pig, Brother Pig, let me come in!"
"Not by the hair of my chinny-chin-chin!"
"I'm the toughest wolf in town!
I'll huff and puff and blow your house down!"

Wolf huffs and puffs with all his might,
But Brother Pig's brick house sits tight.
Wolf tries to huff and puff again,
But the three little pigs just give a grin!
Into the brick house, the pigs won't let Wolf in,
Not by the hair of their chinny-chin-chins!

"The Three Little Pigs" Patterns

"The Three Little Pigs" Patterns (cont.)

"The Three Little Pigs" Patterns *(cont.)*

Straw House

"The Three Little Pigs" Patterns *(cont.)*

Stick House

"The Three Little Pigs" Patterns *(cont.)*

Brick House

Turkey Shapes

Readiness Standards

Fine Motor
- colors, cuts, and pastes

Cognitive
- follows 2- to 3-step directions

Math
- sorts similar objects by size and shape
- understands one-to-one correspondence

Materials
- copy of Turkey Shapes on page 28 for each child
- brown, red, orange, yellow, purple, and dark green construction paper*
- white or light blue paper for background page
- crayons or markers
- scissors and glue
- red chenille stick (optional)

Note: For more varied turkeys, let children cut additional feather triangles using colored-paper scraps.

Teacher Preparation
1. Photocopy the shape patterns onto different-colored construction paper. Color suggestions are provided on the page. You may wish to provide additional colors for the triangular feathers.
2. If appropriate, cut out some or all the shapes ahead of time, and leave each child one or two patterns to cut out. This will save a bit of time but still allow for cutting practice.

Procedure
1. Introduce the project and the components to the group. Explain that they will be creating turkeys using different-sized circular and triangular shapes and that they will be doing it step by step.
2. Hand out the Turkey Shapes and background paper. Assist children as needed with cutting.
3. Glue the larger circle to the middle of the white or light blue paper. Then glue the small circle above the large circle. Explain that this will create the head and body of the turkey.
4. Use two medium triangles for the turkey's feet.
5. Glue the small triangle upside down at the bottom of the smaller circle for the turkey's beak.
6. Use large triangles for the turkey's feathers. Allow children to arrange them as they wish on the body. You may want to encourage them to put an even number of feathers on each side of the turkey's head.
7. Direct the children to finish their turkeys. Remind them to add eyes and a wattle, the fleshy red part under the turkey's chin. (You may choose to glue a piece of chenille stick on the turkey for the wattle.)

  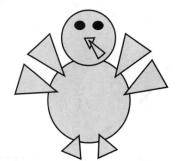

Turkey Shapes *(cont.)*

Turkey Feathers: Copy this strip onto different-colored construction paper. Each child should have at least four different-colored feathers.

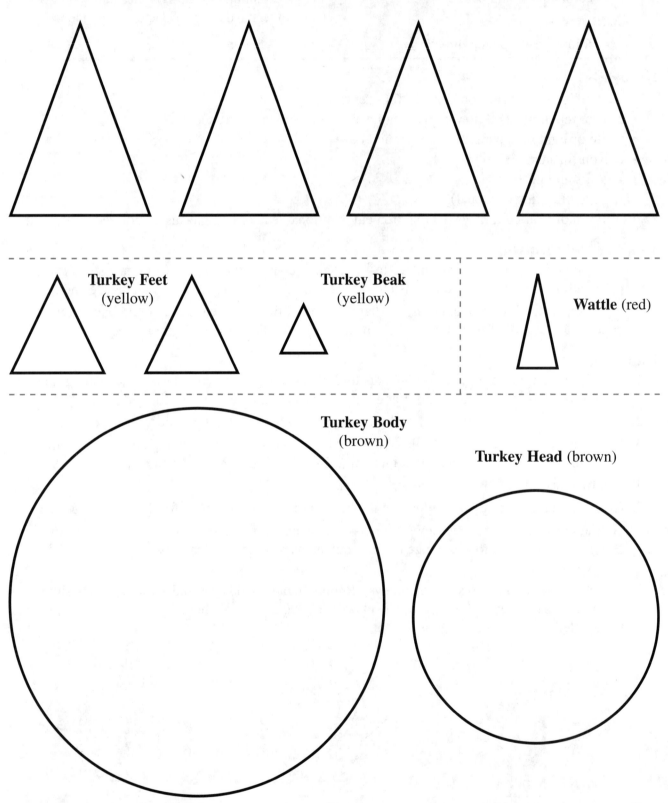

Turkey Feet
(yellow)

Turkey Beak
(yellow)

Wattle (red)

Turkey Body
(brown)

Turkey Head (brown)

Farm Feathers

Readiness Standards

Writing	**Cognitive**	**Fine Motor**
• explores writing letters	• works independently	• works with different textures

Materials

- shallow tray of sand or paint
- examples of farm birds (pictures or books)
- feathers in a variety of sizes, colors, types

    Hint: Feathers are available at craft stores. Purchase the larger flight feathers with stiff nibs to make drawing easier. The softer, downy feathers are difficult to hold or write with and get messy easily.

Procedure

1. Before children go to this center, discuss which farm animals have feathers (birds—*rooster, chicken, turkey, goose, duck*).
2. Show pictures of farm birds. Ask children why they think birds have feathers. *Birds are the only animals that have feathers. Soft feathers keep a bird warm (downy feathers). Stiffer wing feathers help a bird fly, and tail feathers help a bird steer (flight feathers).*
3. Have the children use flight feathers to write in sand or dip in paint to write letters, etc.

Housing Farm Animals

Readiness Standards

Fine Motor	**Social**	**Cognitive**
• stacks blocks	• cooperates with others	• solves problems

Materials

- plastic farm animals
- wooden blocks
- small boxes and other recyclable containers for added interest (i.e., blue plastic lids make great watering holes!)

Procedure

1. Discuss where the farm animals and people live on a farm.
2. Talk about the names for the different locations and discuss which farm animals would live in each.
3. Have the children work together in small groups to create homes for the plastic farm animals using wooden blocks, etc. Suggest building a barn, a pen, a stable, or a chicken coop, depending on which animals are available.

Pigs and Blankets

Readiness Standards

Oral Language
- identifies and sorts pictures into categories

Social
- works together as part of a small group

Cognitive
- understands the spatial concepts *off*, *on*, *over*, and *under*

Materials
- copy of the Pigs and Blankets Cards on page 31 for each pair of children or the color versions, pigs and blankets.pdf, on the CD
- toy pig (Any farm animal may be used to do this activity. Adjust the lesson as needed.)
- facecloth or paper towel
- small toy pig for each pair of children
- small piece of felt, paper towel or tissue for each pair of children

Teacher Preparation
Make copies of the cards for each pair of children. Gather materials to present the activity.

Procedure
1. Review the spatial concepts of *in*, *on*, *over*, and *under* using a toy pig and a facecloth as an example (i.e., This pig is *under* a blanket.).
2. Provide each pair of children with an enlarged set of the Pigs and Blankets Cards. Give each pair of children a toy pig and a piece of felt or tissue and have them perform the actions on the cards using the props.
3. Ask children to take turns demonstrating each spatial concept. Use the pigs or have each child demonstrate using a paper towel or a facecloth.

   - **off** (standing next to the blanket)
   - **on** (sitting on the blanket)

   - **over** (jumping in the air above the blanket)
   - **under** (covered by the blanket)

Pigs and Blankets Cards

How Many Farm Animals?

── Readiness Standards ──

Math
- counts from 1–10; addition
- understands one-to-one correspondence

Oral Language
- uses and understands appropriate vocabulary

Materials
- enlarged Corral Frame pattern (below) or the larger color version, corral.pdf, on the CD
- Farm Animal Counters on page 33 or the color versions, animal counters.pdf, on the CD
- numeral flashcards

Teacher Preparation
1. Make copies of the Corral Frames and Farm Animal Counters for each pair of children. **Note:** Have children color and cut out the patterns the day before if using the black and white versions.
2. Make a large set of 1–10 numeral cards. Gather appropriate materials.

Procedure
1. Give each child a Corral Frame and an appropriate number of Farm Animal Counters. Allow time for children to play with the cards and corrals before introducing the lesson.

2. Place some counters in each child's frame, then show a numeral flashcard and ask, "How many more are needed to make this many?"

3. Have the children place the needed counters on their frames and count to see if they have the correct number.

4. Help each child verbalize what he or she has done. For example, "I had three cows, and I put in three pigs to make six farm animals all together."

Farm Animal Counters

"Old MacDonald Says ..."

Readiness Standards

Gross Motor
- performs gross motor movements

Social
- follows rules

Listening
- listens for a variety of purposes (to perform a task)

Materials
- Old MacDonald Picture Cards below and on page 35 or the color versions, old macdonald cards.pdf, on the CD

Teacher Preparation
1. Color and cut out the Old MacDonald Picture Cards or make color copies. Laminate if possible.

Procedure
1. Explain to the children that they will be playing a game like Simon Says, substituting Old MacDonald's name for Simon's. Remember to add a few commands to the song where children would remain still.

2. Show the children a picture card and begin playing the game.

"Old MacDonald says ..."

- *gallop* like a horse
- *crow* like a rooster
- *paw* the ground like a cat
- *roll* in the mud like a pig

- *strut* like a chicken
- *gobble* like a turkey
- *waddle* like a goose
- *bleat* like a sheep

Old MacDonald Picture Cards

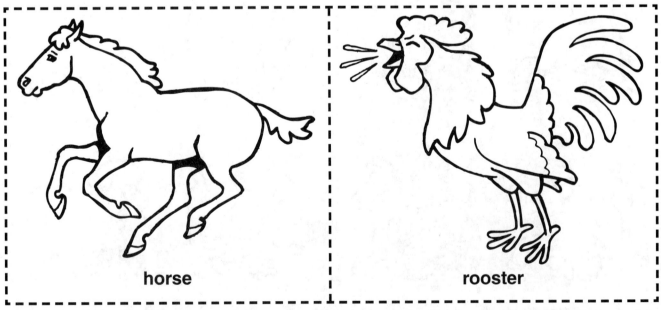

horse

rooster

Old MacDonald Picture Cards *(cont.)*

pig

sheep

chicken

cat

turkey

goose

"The Pigs Go Skipping"

Readiness Standards

Gross Motor
- practices skipping, leaping, hopping, running

Listening
- acts out familiar songs during play

Math
- understands that numbers represent the quantity of objects

Materials
- cardstock
- 4 craft sticks or straws
- Pig Patterns on page 37 or the color versions, pig moves.pdf, on the CD

Teacher Preparation
1. Copy the Pig Patterns onto cardstock to create four pig cards. Label the back of each card: *skipping*, *leaping*, *hopping*, and *dancing*.
2. Use these patterns to create pig stick puppets. (See the directions on page 7.)

Procedure
1. To introduce this song, show the corresponding pig stick puppet with its verse.
2. When the children are familiar with the song, have them perform the actions in groups.
3. For additional math skill practice, instruct children to create a line of each number of pigs while doing the actions (i.e., The pigs go hopping three by three—each line has three children in it).

"The Pigs Go Skipping"

(Sing to the tune of "Ants Go Marching.")

The pigs go **skipping** one by one, oh yes, oh yes!
The pigs go **skipping** one by one, oh yes, oh yes!
The pigs go **skipping** one by one,
The little one stops to beat his drum,
(Pretend to beat on a drum.)

> **Chorus**
> *And they all go **skipping** down to the ground,*
> *To get out of the pen!*
> *Boom! Boom! Boom!*

The pigs go **leaping** two by two, oh yes, oh yes ...
The little one stops to tie his shoe,
(Pretend to tie shoelaces.)

> **Chorus**

The pigs go **hopping** three by three, oh yes, oh yes ...
The little one stops to climb a tree,
(Pretend to climb a tree.)

> **Chorus**

The pigs go **dancing** four by four, oh yes, oh yes ...
The little one stops to shut the door,
(Make a motion like shutting a door.)

> **Chorus**

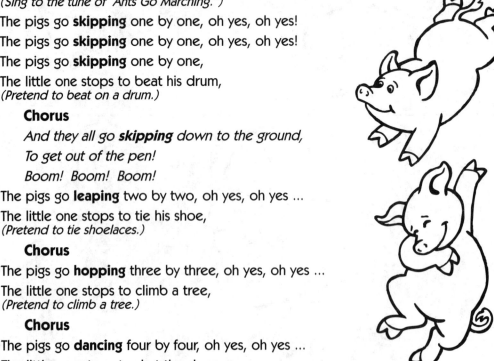

"The Pigs Go Skipping" *(cont.)*

Pig Patterns

Skipping

Hopping

Leaping

Dancing

Souvenir Barn Basket

This is the culminating activity for the farm unit—the take-home souvenir! Assembling this project requires some prep time, depending on the students' cutting abilities. Adult assistance can be helpful and will also provide children with more opportunities to share what they have learned about the farm while working. It is suggested that the barn be assembled on one day and the animals on another.

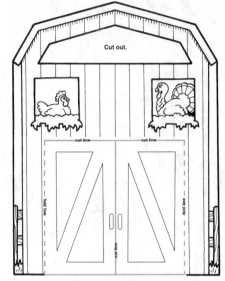

Barn

Materials

- Barn Pattern on page 40 or the back and front color versions, barn patterns.pdf, on the CD
- 2 sheets of heavy red cardstock for each child
- 13.5 oz. cereal box for each child (6.25 x 9.5 front)
- markers or crayons, scissors, glue

Teacher Preparation

1. Copy the Barn Pattern onto red cardstock for each child or make color copies using the patterns for the front and back.
2. Trim the tops of the cereal boxes to measure 7 inches tall.

Barn Front

1. Cut around the border and then cut out the inside of the barn loft window (handle) for each box.
2. Use the pattern as a guide to cut the barn-door opening (solid grey lines) for the front of each box.
3. Cut out the barn doors and fold them (dashed lines) open. This piece will be the front of the barn.

Barn Back

1. Trace the barn template onto another sheet of red cardstock.
2. Cut out the barn loft window (handle).

Procedure

1. Glue the front and back barn patterns onto the cereal box. Try not to get glue on the doors.
2. Fold open the barn doors.

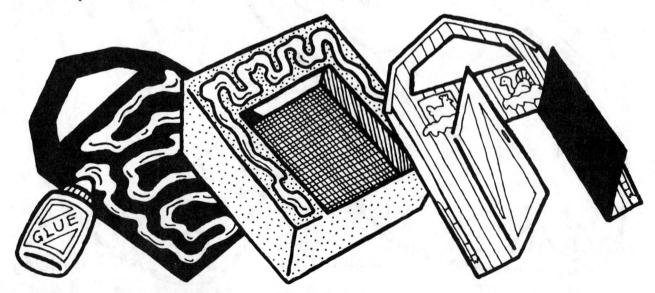

Souvenir Barn Basket (cont.)

Animals

Materials

- Animal Patterns on pages 41–43 for each child, or color versions, folded farm animals.pdf on the CD
- heavy paper or cardstock
- markers or crayons
- cotton balls, scrap paper (optional)

Teacher Preparation

1. Copy the Animal Patterns onto heavy paper for each child to color or make color copies.
2. Cut out the Animal Patterns.
3. Flatten the animal pieces so the children can refold them.

Procedure

1. Fold each animal on the dashed line.
2. Add details to each side of an animal using the materials provided.
3. Try using markers or scrap paper to add spots and udders to the cow and a tail for each animal. Use cotton balls for the sheep's wool and a goatee for the goat.

Souvenir Barn Basket Assembly

Materials

- Barn (see directions on page 38) for each child
- Animals (see directions above) for each child
- School-Home Connection Ticket on page 43 for each child

Teacher Preparation

1. Copy the School-Home Connection Ticket for each child.
2. Gather the completed Barn and Farm Animals projects for each child.

Procedure

1. Place the School-Home Connection Ticket in the barn basket.
2. Walk each animal into the barn.
3. Have children take home the Souvenir Barn Basket to share with family and friends.

School-Home Connection

Making the Barn Basket provides each child with a souvenir of the farm unit to take home to share what he or she has learned. By sending home this handmade souvenir, along with a copy of the School-Home Connection Ticket, each child will be encouraged to discuss what he or she has learned during the unit. Parents can use the prompts on the ticket as a springboard for discussions, songs, stories, and other activities from the farm unit.

Teacher Note: Don't forget to have an official passport stamping at the end of the farm journey.

Souvenir Barn Basket Patterns

Barn Pattern

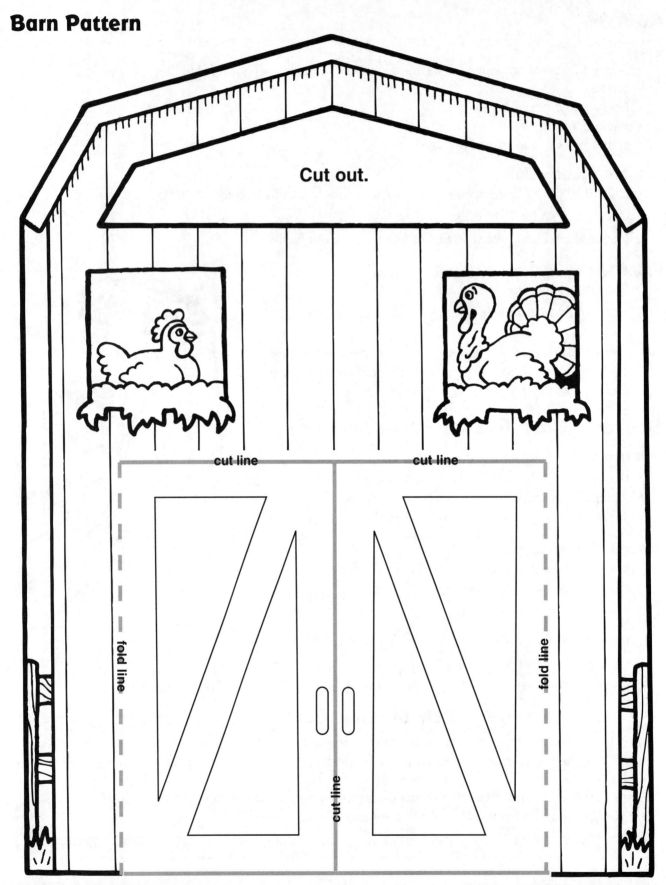

Souvenir Barn Basket Patterns *(cont.)*

Animal Patterns

Directions: Copy the patterns here and on pages 42–43 onto appropriately-colored construction paper. The pattern should be copied on a single folded sheet, with the dotted line of the pattern against the fold.

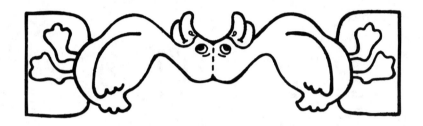

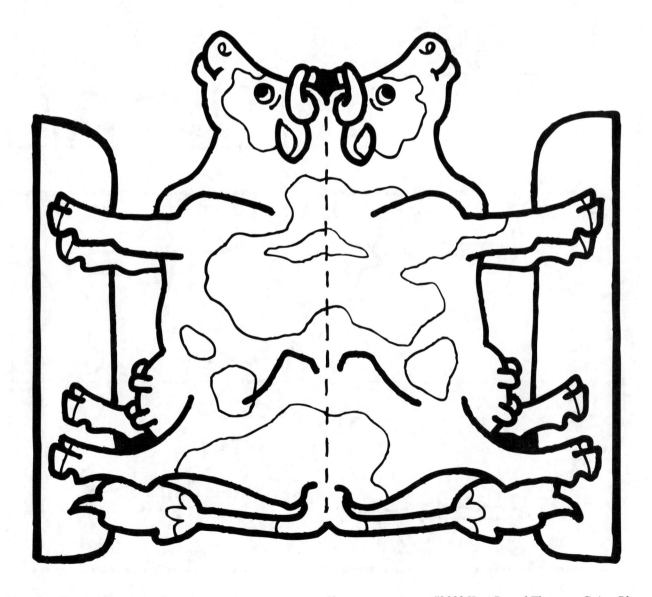

Souvenir Barn Basket Patterns *(cont.)*

Animal Patterns *(cont.)*

Souvenir Barn Basket Patterns (cont.)

Animal Patterns *(cont.)*

School-Home Connection Ticket: Farm

Our class has just finished a study of the farm. Each day we learned more about farms and farm animals. Take a look at your child's Souvenir Barn Basket from our "travels" to the farm. Find out what he or she has learned. Start by discussing which farm animal …

    —is your favorite?

    —makes these sounds: *oink, oink; cluck, cluck; baa, baa; gobble, gobble*; etc.?

    —is brown (pink/white/gray)?

    —has a baby called a piglet (poult/billy/calf)?

    —lives in a pen (barn/coop/stable)?

    —gives us wool (milk/meat/eggs)?

    —has feathers (fur/wool/skin)?

Let's Go to the Pumpkin Patch!

Materials
- Pumpkin Life Cycle Cards on page 47–50 or the color versions, pumpkin life cycle.pdf, on the CD
- Pumpkin Patch Patterns on page 51 or the color versions, pumpkin patch.pdf, on the CD
- pumpkin patch-related items (e.g., real pumpkins, seeds, leaves)
- tray

Teacher Preparation
1. Copy and color class sets of the Pumpkin Life Cycle Cards and Pumpkin Patch Patterns, or make color copies and cut them out.
2. Collect a variety of pumpkin patch-related items (e.g., different colors and/or sizes of real pumpkins, colorful leaves, pumpkin seeds, pumpkin food items) and place them on a tray.

Procedure
1. Have the children sit together in a close group in circle or whole group time. It is important for all children to be able to see the visual aids and hear the responses from classmates.
2. Introduce the unit on the pumpkin patch by presenting the selected visuals, simple questions, and facts about pumpkins and the pumpkin patch.

Where are we going?
Explain to the children that, in their classroom, they will be learning about the pumpkin patch. They will be reading about pumpkin patches and examining pumpkins. They will learn new things that will help them imagine they are part of a real pumpkin patch!

Read a classroom favorite about a pumpkin patch or choose a new book from the Suggested Books listed on page 45. Show the children a collection of pumpkin patch-related items on a tray. Ask them where they think these things are found. *Pumpkins are usually grown on farms or in gardens; a pumpkin grows on a vine from a tiny pumpkin seed.*

Then explain to the children that they will be studying the pumpkin patch. Ask them what they know about the pumpkin patch. *A pumpkin patch is an area on a farm where pumpkins and other crops are grown.* Invite children who have visited a pumpkin patch to briefly describe their experiences.

Who/what will we see at the pumpkin patch?
Ask children who or what they might see at a pumpkin patch. *They might see pumpkins; fall crops, such as apples, gourds, and corn; and farmers and other workers.* Remind children that besides the pumpkins, a pumpkin patch also has people to take care of the crops.

Display the Pumpkin Patch Patterns on a flannel or magnetic board. Discuss the display. Help children brainstorm other things they might see at a pumpkin patch. You may wish to start a chart with pictures and labels. Encourage children to add to it as they learn more about pumpkins. Incorporate the words from the Pumpkin Patch Vocabulary list on page 46 whenever possible. Review these words regularly.

To get started, share the facts provided below about pumpkins.

Pumpkin Facts
- The pumpkin is a fruit, not a vegetable. No two pumpkins are exactly alike!
- Pumpkins are grown all over the world. Pumpkins can grow on six of the seven continents. Antarctica is the only continent where pumpkins will not grow! (For a story about young children who grow pumpkins in Africa, see *One Child, One Seed* in the Suggested Books List on page 45.)
- The pumpkin is a healthful food; it contains vitamin A (helps eyes, skin, teeth, and bones) and vitamin C (helps the body fight infection).

Let's Go to the Pumpkin Patch! *(cont.)*

Procedure *(cont.)*

How does a pumpkin grow?

Display the Pumpkin Life Cycle Cards sequentially on the board to show how a pumpkin grows from a seed. Explain to the children that a pumpkin seed needs three things to grow: *sun, water,* and *soil.* Remind the children that pumpkins grow on vines. It's also a good idea to give pumpkins a lot of space to grow because some can get very large! Explain the pumpkin's life cycle:

1. First a pumpkin seed is planted in the soil. A pumpkin grows in approximately 120 days. To harvest a pumpkin by October, it needs to be planted in June.

2. Then the pumpkin seed sprouts. At the same time the pumpkin sprout is growing above the ground, roots are growing below the soil. Pumpkin roots have thin tubes. They suck up water from the ground like you might use a straw to drink water.

3. The pumpkin sprout becomes a plant, with green leaves and tendrils.

4. A yellow flower blossom appears on the plant.

5. The blossom withers. Female flowers become little pumpkins.

6. The green pumpkin grows larger, changing colors from green to yellow, then orange.

7. Now, the pumpkin may be cut from the vine and enjoyed.

What could we do at the pumpkin patch?

Ask children about how they might use each of the five senses when observing the pumpkin patch. They might *see* a green vine, *hear* crows cawing, *taste* roasted pumpkin seeds, *touch* a bumpy pumpkin, and *smell* damp soil.

When is the best time to visit the pumpkin patch?

Ask children when they would visit a pumpkin patch. *A good time to visit a pumpkin patch to see pumpkins growing or harvested would be fall.*

What type of clothes would you wear?

Ask children what they should wear on the visit to the pumpkin patch. *A pumpkin patch is outdoors. Pumpkins are often harvested in October. You might choose to wear a jacket, shirt, and long pants to stay warm. It is a good idea to wear sturdy boots or shoes, too.*

Why would you like to visit the pumpkin patch?

Invite children to give reasons why they would like to visit a pumpkin patch. *You could see where pumpkins grow, the different parts of the pumpkin plant, and the animals and equipment that might be part of the pumpkin patch.*

Suggested Books

Five Little Pumpkins by Iris Van Rynbach

From Seed to Pumpkin by Wendy Pfeffer

One Child, One Seed by Kathryn Cave

Plumply, Dumply Pumpkin by Mary Serfozo

The Pumpkin Book by Gail Gibbons

The Pumpkin Fair by Eve Bunting

Pumpkin Heads! by Wendell Minor

Pumpkin Jack by Will Hubbell

Pumpkin Pumpkin by Jeanne Titherington

Sixteen Runaway Pumpkins by Dianne Ochiltree

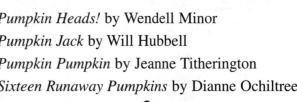

Pumpkin Patch Vocabulary

Life Cycle

blossom	plant	seed	tendrils
flower	pollinate	skin	vine
fruit	pumpkin	soil	water
grow	ripe	sprout	
leaf	rotten	stem	
nectar	rows	sun	

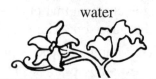

Shapes and Sizes

circle	round
huge	short
large	small
medium	sphere
mini	tall
oval	tiny

Textures

bumpy	shiny
gooey	smooth
hard	soft
prickly	squishy
ribbed	wrinkled
rough	

Pumpkin Seed Information

Small Pumpkins
(less than 1 pound)
Baby Boo (white)
Jack-Be-Little
Munchkin
Sweetie Pie

Giant Pumpkins
(more than 100 pounds)
Atlantic Giant
Big Max
Big Moon
Prizewinner

For Eating
(3–8 pounds)
New England Pie
Spooktacular
Triple Treat
Winter Luxury

For Carving
(10–40 pounds)
Autumn Gold
Casper (white)
Jumpin' Jack
Trick or Treat

Colors

brown	orange	tan	yellow
green	red	white	

Foods

bread	pancakes
butter	pie
cookies	pudding
ice cream	seeds
muffins	soup

Jack-o'-Lanterns

carve	light
face	scoop
glow	spooky
grin	triangle
hollow	zigzag

Pumpkin Life Cycle Cards

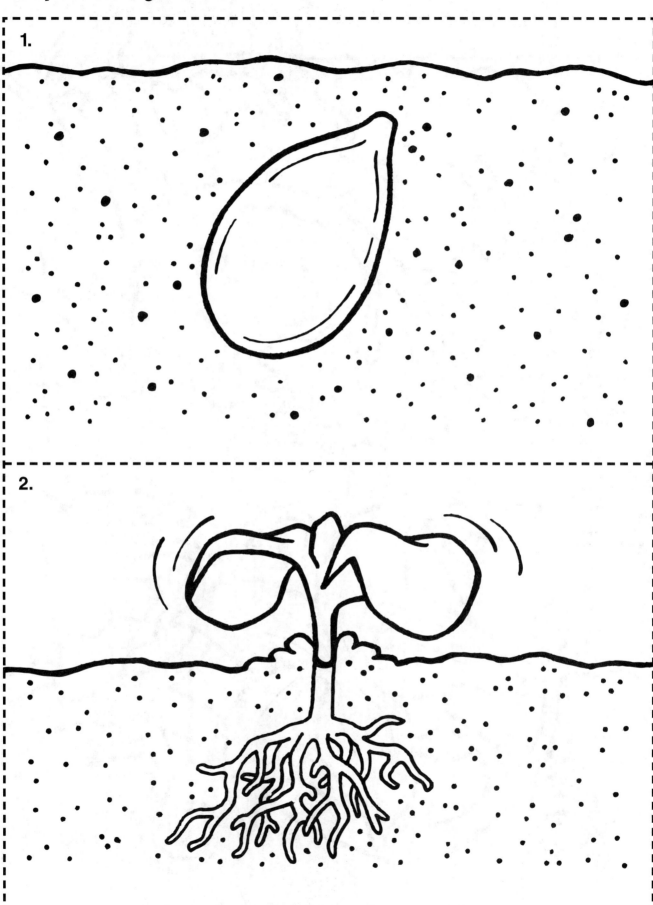

1.

2.

Pumpkin Life Cycle Cards *(cont.)*

3.

4.

Pumpkin Life Cycle Cards *(cont.)*

5.

6.

Pumpkin Life Cycle Cards *(cont.)*

7.

8.

Pumpkin Patch Patterns

trowel

gloves

pruning
shears

planter

"The Little Black Crow"

Readiness Standards

Reading
- understands top-to-bottom directionality
- knows elements of a story (e.g., *setting*)
- knows some familiar words in print (e.g., *I, me*)
- relates story to his or her own life experience
- predicts story outcome using prior knowledge

Materials
- "The Little Black Crow" rhyming story poster on pages 54–55 or the color version, crow story.pdf, on the CD
- "The Little Black Crow" Cards on pages 56–61 or the color versions, crow story cards.pdf, on the CD
- craft sticks or straws
- markers
- tape

Teacher Preparation
1. Color, cut out, and laminate the story cards. Attach each pattern to a craft stick using tape to create character puppets.

2. Spend a few days immersing students in this rhyming variation of "The Little Red Hen" story.

3. Read the rhyming story "The Little Black Crow." The more you read the story to the children, the more they will be familiar with it and the more they will be able to participate.
   - **Preview** new vocabulary, such as *scurrying, route, twine, pup, soaring,* and *scrumptious,* with the children. (**Note:** In this rhyming story, the vowel sound in the word *route* is pronounced "ow" as in the word *cow.*)
   - **Discuss/Practice** the refrains: "Who will help?" "Not I." "I will!"

Procedure
1. Share with the children the book, "The Little Red Hen," or briefly review the main events in the familiar tale:
   - The hen *plants* the wheat by herself. The wheat grows tall.
   - The hen *cuts* the wheat by herself.
   - The hen *threshes* the wheat by herself.
   - The hen *takes* the wheat to the mill by herself.
   - The hen *makes* and *bakes* the bread by herself.
   - Although the duck, cat, and dog have not helped at all, they still want to eat the bread. However, the Little Red Hen says that she will *eat the bread by herself,* and she does!

2. Explain to the children that you will be reading a rhyming story about another animal who asks for help. Introduce the main characters in "The Little Black Crow": Crow, Scarecrow, Squirrel, and Bat. Show the children a stick puppet of each character.

3. Hand out the character stick puppets for the first stanza of the rhyming story. Explain to the children that some of them will hold up the corresponding stick puppet as the story unfolds.

"The Little Black Crow" *(cont.)*

Procedure *(cont.)*

4. Read the first stanza of "The Little Black Crow" rhyming story to the group. Instruct a child to hold up a character puppet as it is mentioned.

5. Collect the stick puppets from the first group of children. Hand out the character stick puppets to a second group of children for the second stanza of the rhyming story.

6. Continue in this manner until reaching the last two lines of the story. Ask the children what they think the Little Black Crow will do with the pumpkin pie. Remind them to think of what happened in the familiar tale, "The Little Red Hen."

7. Read the remainder of the rhyming story. Review the children's predictions and discuss the actual outcome of the story.

Revisiting the Rhyming Story

Once children are familiar with the rhyming story, "The Little Black Crow," try the following activities:

1. Point to each line and icon on the rhyming story poster pages as you read what the character says. Emphasize to the children that you start at the top of the page and continue reading to the bottom of the page.

2. Ask students which word is repeated throughout the rhyming story. (*I*) Have several students take turns pointing to the word *I* on the rhyming story poster.

3. Ask the children where the story of "The Little Black Crow" happens. (*pumpkin patch*) Have them explain how they know this.

For example:

A child might say, "I know this story happens in a pumpkin patch because ..."

- a pumpkin seed is planted.
- a pumpkin grows on a vine.
- animals that you might see at a pumpkin patch are in the story.

Character Concept

Crow worked hard to plant, harvest, and prepare a pumpkin to bake a homemade pumpkin pie. That was a big job for one little bird! Unfortunately, Scarecrow, Squirrel, and Bat did not want to help. How could this job have been made easier/quicker/more enjoyable? *If all the animals had cooperated, they could have worked together and broke a big job into smaller parts.*

Direct the children to think about a time when someone helped them. Invite several children to share how it made them feel when they were helped by others.

"The Little Black Crow"

 Crow: Who will help plant this pumpkin seed?

 Scarecrow: Not I, I'm going to rest indeed!

 Squirrel: Not I, I'm burying what I need.

 Bat: Not I, I'm flying with great speed.

 Crow: Who will help water the pumpkin sprout?

 Scarecrow: Not I, I'm going to stand and pout.

 Squirrel: Not I, I'm scurrying all about.

 Bat: Not I, I'm taking a different route.

 Crow: Who will help pick it off the vine?

 Scarecrow: Not I, I'm busy holding a sign.

 Squirrel: Not I, I'm gathering pieces of twine.

 Bat: Not I, I'm hanging from a tall line.

Crow: Who will help mash the pumpkin up?

 Scarecrow: Not I, I'm watching a playful pup.

 Squirrel: Not I, I'm collecting nuts in a cup.

 Bat: Not I, I'm looking for bugs to scoop up.

 Crow: Who will help bake the pumpkin pie?

 Scarecrow: Not I, I'm much too lazy a guy.

 Squirrel: Not I, I'm much too busy to try.

 Bat: Not I, I'm soaring much too high.

 Crow: Who would like to help me eat?

 Scarecrow: I will! Pumpkin pie can't be beat.

 Squirrel: I will! What a scrumptious treat.

 Bat: I will! Pie is better than meat.

 Crow: Too bad for you, I will eat it all.

Next time, please help me when I call!

"The Little Black Crow" Cards

Crow planting a seed

Scarecrow resting

Squirrel burying what he needs

Bat flying with speed

"The Little Black Crow" Cards *(cont.)*

Crow watering a sprout

Scarecrow pouting

Squirrel scurrying

Bat changing direction

"The Little Black Crow" Cards *(cont.)*

Crow picking a pumpkin

Scarecrow holding a sign

Squirrel playing with twine

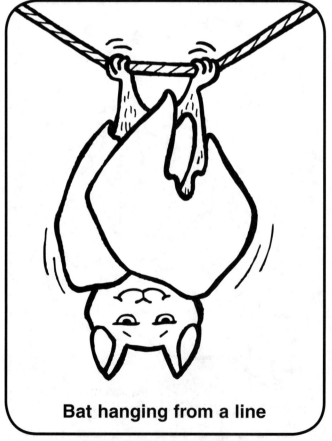

Bat hanging from a line

"The Little Black Crow" Cards *(cont.)*

Crow mashing up pumpkin

Scarecrow watching a puppy

Squirrel collecting nuts

Bat diving to catch a bug

"The Little Black Crow" Cards *(cont.)*

Crow baking a pie in the oven

Scarecrow being lazy

Squirrel acting busy

Bat soaring high

"The Little Black Crow" Cards *(cont.)*

**Crow holding up a
steaming slice of pie**

Scarecrow nodding, yes!

Squirrel nodding, yes!

Bat nodding, yes!

I Spy a Pumpkin

═══ Readiness Standards ═══

Social
- recognizes and describes emotions
- takes turns

Oral Language
- speaks clearly
- follows conversation rules (e.g., staying on topic)

Materials

- "If Your Pumpkin …" Patterns on page 79
- Pumpkin Spy Mask Patterns on page 63 or the color version, pumpkin masks.pdf, on the CD
- plastic straw for each pair of children
- cardstock
- markers
- tape

Teacher Preparation

1. Copy, color, and cut out the "If Your Pumpkin …" Patterns and the Pumpkin Spy Mask for each pair of children or make color copies. **Note:** All the pumpkins should be the same color since the focus is on the emotions in this activity.
2. Attach a straw to the back of one side of each Pumpkin Spy Mask.
3. Place the pumpkin patterns and spy mask at a center.

Procedure

1. Review with the children different emotions (e.g., angry, tired, sad, worried, happy, surprised). Have them act out feeling these emotions.
2. Children visit the center in pairs. One wears the Pumpkin Spy Mask and says the phrase, "I spy with my pumpkin eyes, a pumpkin that is (type of emotion)." The child wearing the mask describes a pumpkin. For example, "I see a pumpkin that is angry. It has no stem."

3. The second child guesses which pumpkin the other child is describing and then points to the appropriate pumpkin. If correct, the child is complimented by his partner. If incorrect, the child wearing the mask gives another hint about that pumpkin.
4. When a pumpkin is guessed correctly, it gets "picked" and set aside.
5. The second child dons the Pumpkin Spy Mask and repeats steps 2–4 for the first child.
6. The pair continues in this manner until all the pumpkins have been accurately described.

Pumpkin Spy Mask Patterns

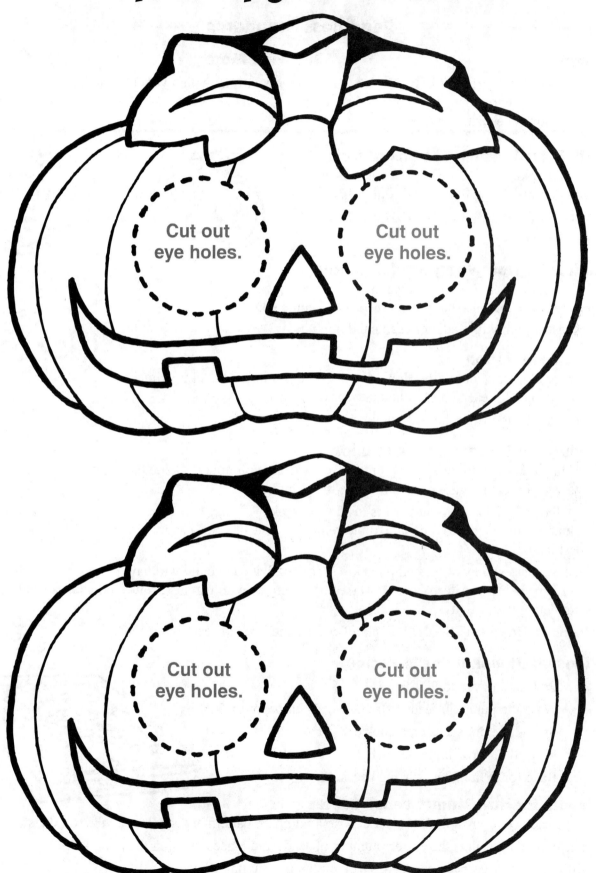

How Many Seeds?

Readiness Standards

Math

- recognizes groups (sets) of one, two, three, four, five, and six objects
- knows the written numerals, 1–6

Fine Motor

- works with a variety of textures

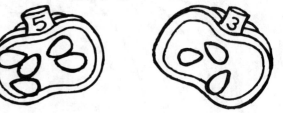

Materials for Teacher Demonstration

- real pumpkin
- knife (adult use only)
- large spoon or scoop
- paper towels
- cookie sheet
- salt
- oven
- plastic cloth

Materials for How Many Seeds? Center

- How Many Seeds? Pumpkin Patterns on page 65 or the color versions, how many seeds.pdf, on the CD
- 6 roasted pumpkin seeds for each child

Teacher Preparation

1. Copy, color, and cut out the How Many Seeds? Pumpkin Patterns or make color copies for each child. Laminate for durability.
2. Remove the top from the real pumpkin.

Procedure for Teacher Demonstration

1. During whole group time, scoop out the seeds from a pumpkin. Invite the children to carefully observe you gathering seeds from inside the pumpkin.
2. Ask the children to tell you what is inside a pumpkin. (*pulp, stringy stuff, fruit, seeds*) Allow volunteers to reach into the pumpkin to remove the seeds. Set aside the seeds to clean and roast later.
3. Make a class supply of toasted pumpkin seeds, so that each child will have at least six seeds. (See the recipe below.) **Allergy Note:** Make sure to check with parents about food allergies before completing this activity.
4. Place the How Many Seeds? Pumpkin Patterns and roasted seeds at a center.

Toasted Pumpkin Seeds Recipe

a. Preheat an oven to 300°F.

b. Wash the pumpkin seeds. Dry the seeds on paper towels.

c. Spread the dry seeds on a cookie sheet.

d. If desired, sprinkle the seeds lightly with salt.

e. Bake for 30 minutes, stirring occasionally.

Procedure for How Many Seeds? Center

1. Have each child visiting the center choose a pumpkin pattern and say the number on the stem.
2. The child then counts the correct number of seeds and places them on the pumpkin.
3. After the work has been checked, snack on the real pumpkin seeds!

How Many Seeds? Pumpkin Patterns

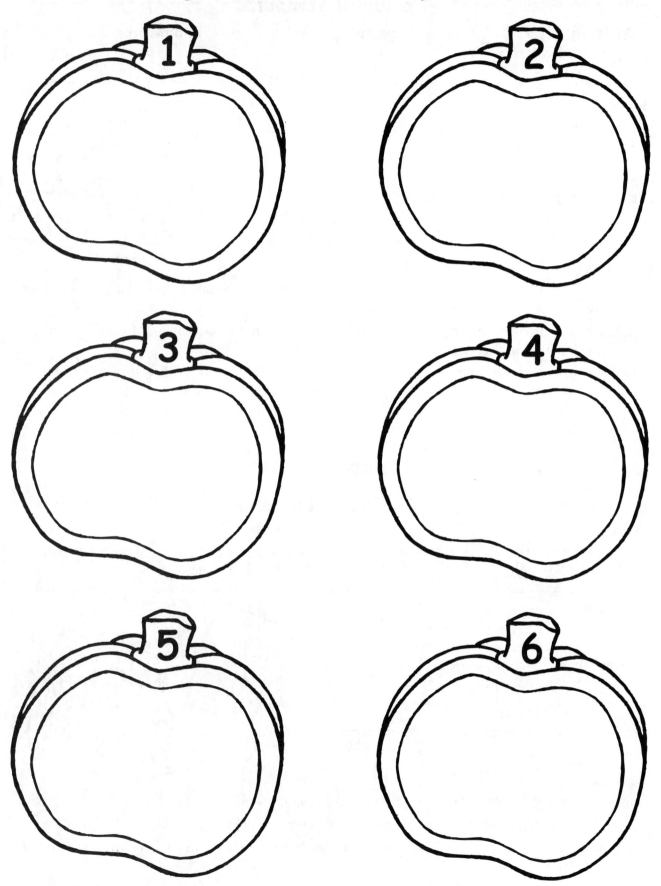

"A-dough-able" Pumpkin Museum

Readiness Standards

Writing
- practices tracing words

Cognitive
- solves problems

Fine Motor
- creates objects using play dough

Materials
- small piece of cardstock for each child
- orange play dough
- pencil

Teacher Preparation
1. Fold the small pieces of cardstock to make name cards.
2. Gather materials for the activity and place them at a center.

Procedure
1. Children visit a center and create a variety of pumpkins with the orange play dough. Have them make some big pumpkins and some little pumpkins.
2. Each child chooses the pumpkin he or she likes best and thinks of a name that fits that pumpkin (e.g., Goliath, Big Daddy, Teeny, Baby Boo), depending on its size!
3. The teacher writes the pumpkin's name in large letters on a piece of cardstock, and the child traces the letters in the word, using a pencil or other writing implement.
4. Create a Pumpkin Museum by displaying each pumpkin with its name card. Provide time for the children to take a peek at the pumpkins in the museum!

Pumpkin Hunt

Readiness Standards

Math
- understands that numbers represent a quantity of objects

Cognitive
- attends to adult-directed tasks for short periods of time

Materials
- numeral flashcards (1–5)
- at least 5 pumpkin novelty erasers
- assortment of novelty erasers
- small bin or container

Teacher Preparation
Gather an assortment of novelty erasers, including at least five pumpkin novelty erasers, and place them in a small bin.

Procedure
1. Give a numeral flashcard to each student in the group.
2. Tell each child to collect the correct number of pumpkin erasers from a bin of novelty erasers.
3. Check children's work, then have them return the pumpkin erasers to the bin and switch or trade numeral cards.

Shapely Jack-o'-Lantern

── Readiness Standards ──

Math
- knows basic geometric language for naming shapes (e.g., rectangle, square)

Fine Motor
- colors and pastes

Cognitive
- follows 2- or 3-step directions
- understands the spatial concepts *below*, *above*, *middle*, and *beside*

Materials
- Shapely Jack-o'-Lantern Patterns on pages 68–69 or the color versions, pumpkin.pdf, on the CD
- variety of materials to embellish product (scraps of paper, yarn, glitter)
- 3 real pumpkins (1 small, 1 medium, 1 large)
- black construction paper

Note: This center works best with a small group of children and an adult giving the oral directions to complete the art project.

Teacher Preparation
1. Copy, color, and cut out the pumpkin on page 68 or make a color copy of the pumpkin.
2. Trace the Pumpkin Features onto black paper and cut them out.
3. Provide a pumpkin and features for each child.

Procedure
1. Review the spatial concepts of *below*, *above*, *middle*, and *beside* using real pumpkins as an example (i.e., The big pumpkin is *beside* the little pumpkin. The large pumpkin is *in the middle*.).
2. Provide each child with a set of the Shapely Jack-o'-Lantern Patterns.
3. Give the children directions to complete the Shapely Jack-o'-Lantern:
   a   Glue the square on the middle of the pumpkin for a nose.
   b.   Choose 2 rhombus (diamonds) or 2 triangles. Glue one shape above the nose. Glue the second one beside the first. (eyes)
   c.   Choose a rectangle or an oval. Glue it above the eyes for a stem.
   d.   Glue one oval below the nose for a mouth.
   e.   You may use the leftover shapes to decorate your pumpkin. Personalize your Shapely Jack-o'-Lantern by adding hair, ears, eyewear, etc.

Shapely Jack-o'-Lantern Patterns

Pumpkin

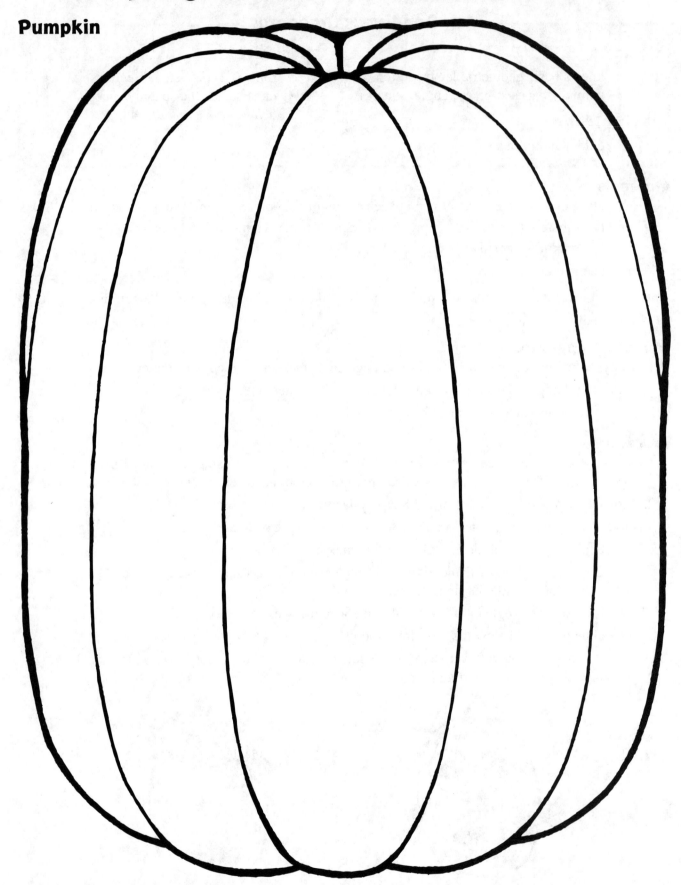

Shapely Jack-o'-Lantern Patterns *(cont.)*

Pumpkin Features

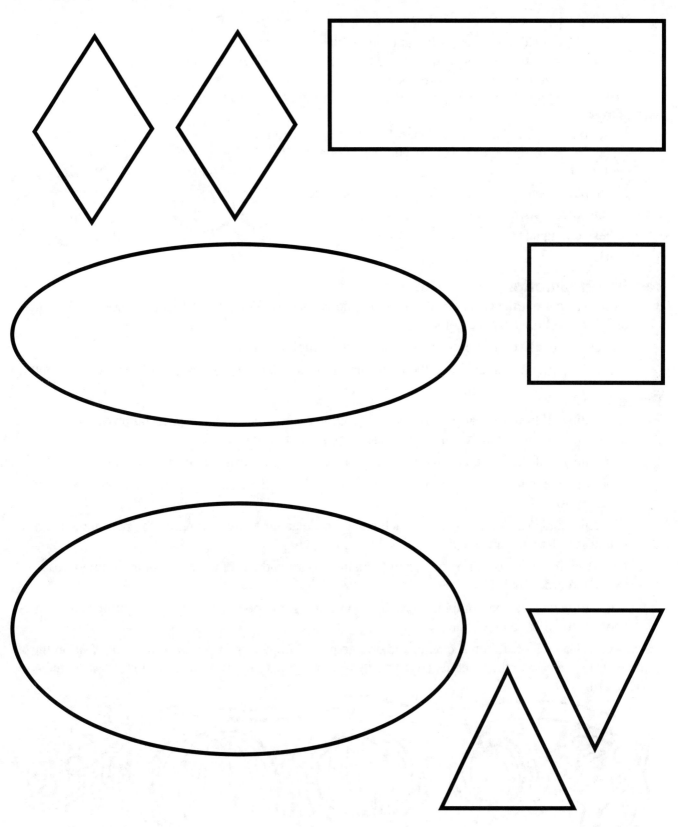

Order on the Vine!

Readiness Standards

Math

- orders objects by measurable attribute (e.g., smallest to largest, shortest to tallest)
- understands one-to-one correspondence

Cognitive

- solves problems
- works independently

Materials

- Order on the Vine! Game Board and Pumpkin Patterns on pages 71–72 or the color versions, vine game board.pdf, on the CD
- 3 pumpkins (variety of sizes: small, medium, large)
- cookie sheet or small magnetic board
- adhesive magnets
- markers

Teacher Preparation

1. Copy and cut out the Order on the Vine! Game Board and Pumpkin Patterns. Color *Set A* orange and *Set B* yellow or make color copies.
2. Attach an adhesive magnet to the back of each Pumpkin Pattern.
3. Place the pumpkin patterns and the Order on the Vine! Game Board on a cookie sheet at a center.

Procedure

1. Show the children the real pumpkins. Ask volunteers to tell the class which pumpkin is the smallest. Which one is the largest? the shortest? the tallest?
2. With the aid of the class, arrange the real pumpkins in order from smallest to largest.
3. Working independently, a child visits the center and uses the orange pumpkin patterns (*Set A*) to order by size.
4. The child attaches one pumpkin to each stem on the game board, arranging the pumpkins from smallest to largest on the vine.
5. He or she removes the pumpkins from the game board and uses the yellow pumpkin patterns (*Set B*) to order by height.
6. The child attaches one pumpkin to each stem on the game board, arranging the pumpkins from shortest to tallest on the vine.

Variations: Have the children sequence the orange pumpkin patterns from *largest* to *smallest* on the game board. Then have them sequence the yellow pumpkin patterns from *tallest* to *shortest* on the game board.

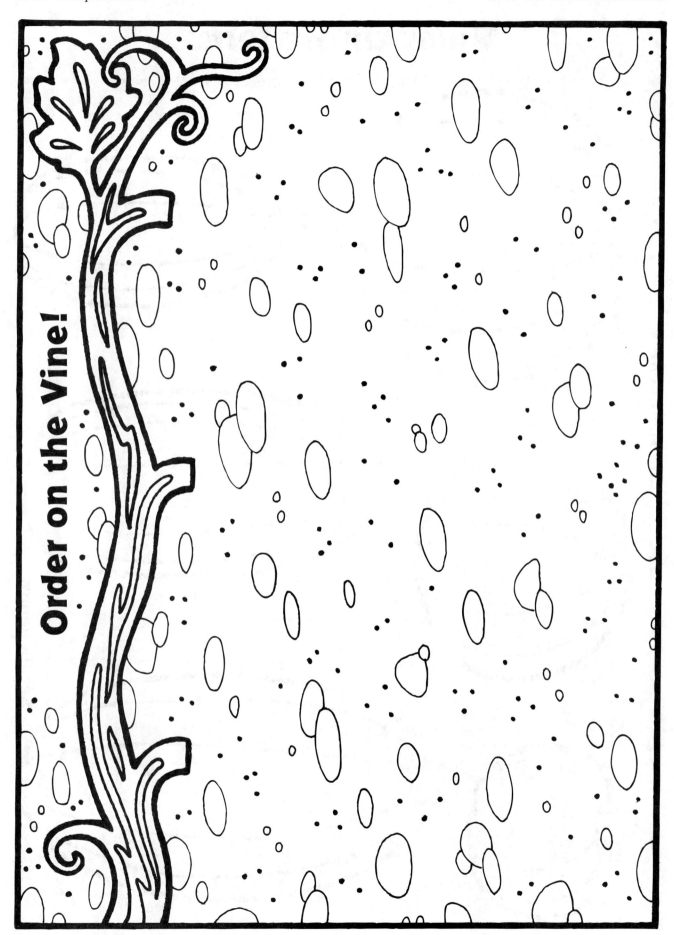

Order on the Vine!

Pumpkin Patterns

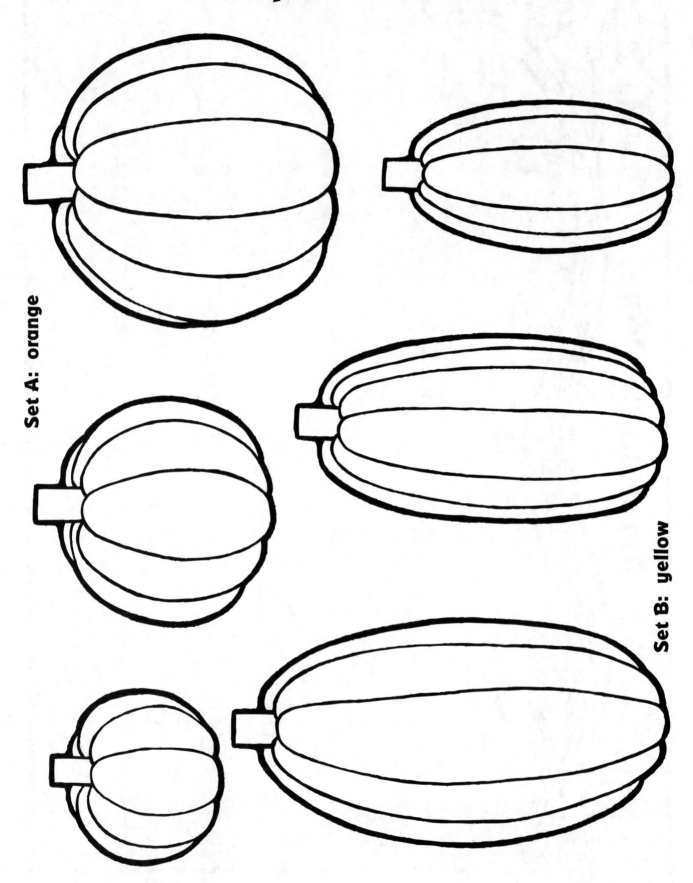

Pretend Pumpkin Muffins

Readiness Standards

Social
- shares with others

Fine Motor
- works with a variety of kitchen tools

Materials
- Pumpkin Muffin Recipe Cards on page 74 or the color versions, recipe cards.pdf, on the CD

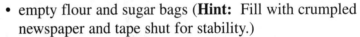

Cooking and Dining Tools
- aprons
- cookie scoops
- measuring cups
- measuring spoons
- mixing bowls
- muffin liners
- muffin pans
- rolling pins
- small cups
- small plates
- spoons
- whisks

Ingredients
Empty Boxes/Cartons
- egg cartons
- milk cartons
- cinnamon container
- ginger container
- baking soda box
- baking powder container
- empty flour and sugar bags (**Hint:** Fill with crumpled newspaper and tape shut for stability.)
- empty canned pumpkin (**Hint:** Make sure there are no sharp edges on the cans. Tape the lids back on.)

Safety Note: Use tin, metal, plastic or other unbreakable materials, not glass or ceramic containers.

Allergy Note: Even coming into contact with *empty* ingredient boxes and cartons can cause reactions in children with food allergies. Check with parents for food allergies before the activity.

Teacher Preparation
1. Copy, color, and cut out the Pumpkin Recipe Cards.
2. Gather a variety of kitchen and dining tools and empty ingredient boxes/cartons, bags, and cans for your dramatic play area or kitchen center.

Procedure
1. Review with the children the steps to make pumpkin muffins. Model the steps below and the activity shown on each recipe card.
2. Pretend to make muffins using the Pumpkin Muffin Recipe Cards, kitchen tools, and supplies.

   a. *Gather* ingredients for the recipe.
   b. *Measure* the ingredients using kitchen tools.
   c. *Pour* the ingredients into a bowl and *blend* using a spoon.
   d. *Place* muffin liners in a muffin pan. *Scoop* the pretend pumpkin muffin batter into individual liners.
   e. *Bake* the muffins in a pretend oven.
   f. *Take* the muffins out and let cool.
   g. *Serve* the pretend pumpkin muffins on a small plate.
   h. *Pour* pretend milk into a small cup to drink!

Pumpkin Muffin Recipe Cards

1 Measure

2 Blend

3 Scoop

4 Bake

Friendship Pumpkin

━━ Readiness Standards ━━

Social
- works together as part of a group
- compliments others

Gross Motor
- rolls a ball to a target (another person)

Oral Language
- uses appropriate vocabulary (e.g., compliments)
- speaks understandably

Materials
- ball of orange yarn or orange ball
- orange poster board
- marker
- green construction paper
- Shapely Jack-O'-Latern Pumpkin Pattern on page 68 or the color version, pumpkin.pdf, on the CD

Teacher Preparation
1. Prepare a large pumpkin cutout using poster board. Enlarge the pumpkin pattern or use the color version, on the CD.
2. Cut out pumpkin leaves for each child. Use the Pumpkin Leaves Patterns on page 84 or the color versions, pumpkin leaves.pdf, on the CD.
3. Beforehand, explain to the children that kindness and trying to get along with others is important.
4. Give examples of appropriate compliments children can share with one another. (*It was nice of you to help me clean up the blocks.*)

Procedure
1. Gather the children in a circle on the floor.
2. Have a child start the game by rolling the Friendship Pumpkin (orange ball of yarn) to a teacher.
3. The teacher then gives a compliment to the child who rolled the yarn ball to him or her, holds the "pumpkin," and rolls it to another child.
4. The teacher records the compliment given on the child's leaf and the child adds the leaf to the large pumpkin cutout to create a Friendship Pumpkin.
5. Repeat rolling the Friendship Pumpkin in the same manner until all the children have received a compliment to add to the friendship pumpkin cutout.
6. The last child rolls the Friendship Pumpkin back to the teacher, who then gives him or her a compliment.
7. Display the large Friendship Pumpkin, full of compliments, where the children can see it. Refer often to the Friendship Pumpkin, reminding children of words they can use to show their kindness with one another.

"Five Little Pumpkins" Fingerplay

Readiness Standards

Math
- counts from 1 to 5

Listening
- listens for a variety of purposes (e.g., to learn what happened in a story; to follow directions)

Fine and Gross Motor
- performs fine-motor movements
- performs gross-motor movements (e.g., run, roll)

Materials
- Five Little Pumpkins Patterns on page 77 or the color versions, five pumpkins.pdf, on the CD
- glove (cloth gardening glove)
- fabric glue

Teacher Preparation
1. Copy, color, and cut out the "Five Little Pumpkins" Patterns or make color copies.
2. Glue the gate to the base of the glove.
3. Glue one pumpkin on each finger of the glove to make a glove puppet.

Procedure
1. Practice "Five Little Pumpkins" (below) with the children. Perform the finger actions as you go through the poem.
2. Encourage the children to hold up their corresponding fingers as you recite the poem again. Have them roll on the ground after the last refrain!
3. Later invite the children to take turns pretending to be each of the five pumpkins and performing the actions. For example, after the fifth line, have a child run in place.

"Five Little Pumpkins"

Five little pumpkins sitting on a gate,
(Hold up all five pumpkins on glove.)

The **first** one said, "Oh my, it's getting late."
(Point to the pumpkin on the first finger.)

The **second** one said, "There are bats in the air."
(Wiggle or point to the pumpkin on the second finger.)

The **third** one said, "I don't care."
(Wiggle or point to the pumpkin on the third finger.)

The **fourth** one said, "Let's run, run, run."
(Wiggle or point to the pumpkin on fourth finger.)

The **fifth** one said, "Let's roll and have some fun!"
(Hold up pumpkin on fifth finger. Roll entire hand as if all pumpkins are rolling!)

Five Little Pumpkins Patterns

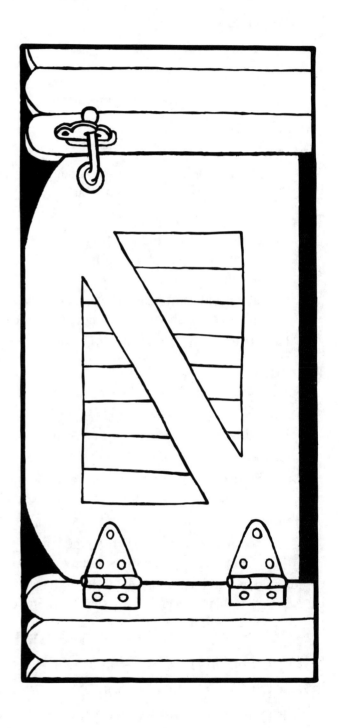

"If Your Pumpkin ..."

Readiness Standards

Cognitive
- recognizes and identifies colors

Gross Motor
- performs gross-motor movements

Social
- recognizes emotions

Math
- sorts objects by attribute (e.g., color, size, shape)

Materials
- "If Your Pumpkin ..." Patterns on pages 79–81 or the color versions, if your pumpkin.pdf, on the CD
- hole punch
- yarn

Teacher Preparation
1. Copy, color, and cut out the "If Your Pumpkin ..." Patterns or make color copies and a set of black and white pumpkins. If using the black-and-white version, make two copies of page 79 for the white/blue pumpkins.
2. Create a necklace for each child, using a different "If Your Pumpkin ..." Pattern as a medallion. Use the hole punch to punch a hole (as indicated) and thread a length of yarn through the pattern.
3. Distribute an "If Your Pumpkin ..." necklace to each child.

Procedure
1. Slowly read aloud the "If Your Pumpkin ..." poem below. (Pause after naming each color to give the children a chance to get ready for the appropriate action.)
2. Have the children switch necklaces and repeat step 1.
3. Continue in this manner for a desired amount of time.

Variation: Have the children participate in a Pumpkin Parade! Give verbal directions using the pumpkin necklaces for lining three children up at a time.

Example:

"The orange pumpkin goes first, the huge pumpkin goes second, and the oval pumpkin goes last."
"The sad pumpkin is first, the happy pumpkin is second, and the angry pumpkin is last."

Children may also be encouraged to form their own parade groups by sorting their pumpkin necklaces by color, size, shape, face/no face, stem/no stem, etc.

"If Your Pumpkin ..."

If your pumpkin is *white*—run in place with all your might.

If your pumpkin is *blue*—shout out a very loud, "Boo!"

If your pumpkin is *tan*—wave your arms like a fan.

If your pumpkin is *yellow*—shake like a bowl full of Jello®.

If your pumpkin is *green*—make the scariest face you've ever seen.

If your pumpkin is *red*—rub the top of your head.

If your pumpkin is *orange*, so bright—pretend to be a bat in flight!

"If Your Pumpkin ..." *(cont.)*

Blue – Make an additional set and keep it white.

Tan

"If Your Pumpkin ..." (cont.)

Patterns (cont.)

Yellow

Green

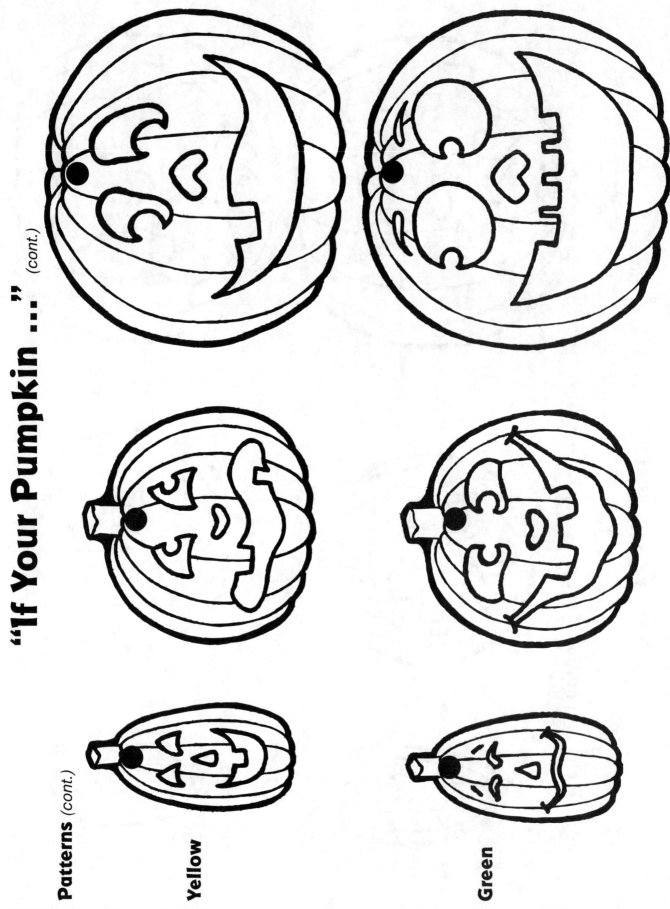

"If Your Pumpkin ..." (cont.)

Patterns (cont.)

Red

Orange

Souvenir Pumpkin Pal

This is the culminating activity for the pumpkin patch unit—the take-home souvenir! Assembling this project requires some prep time, depending on the students' abilities. Adult assistance can be helpful, and will also provide children with more opportunities to share what they have learned about the pumpkin patch while they are working. It is suggested that the pumpkin project be assembled on one day and the *My Pumpkin Pal* book on another.

Pumpkin

Materials
- Pumpkin Leaves Patterns on page 84 or the color versions, pumpkin leaves.pdf, on the CD
- 8 oz. empty, small plastic water bottle (pod style) with cap for each child
- approximately six 12" strips of orange crepe paper for each child
- 12" green chenille stick for each child
- green construction paper
- brown tempera paint
- paintbrushes
- glue and scissors

Teacher Preparation
1. Copy the Pumpkin Leaves Patterns onto green construction paper. Cut two leaves for each child or make color copies.
2. Remove the caps from the plastic bottles and set them aside.

Procedure
1. To create this petite pumpkin, glue a crepe paper strip on the bottle (at the top), glue it beneath the bottle, and then glue it to the opposite side. (**Teacher Note:** You may wish to have children paint the entire bottle with glue before attaching the crepe paper strips. Suggest they steady the glue-covered bottle by putting the index finger of one hand inside the bottle when holding it.)
2. Continue in this manner with the remaining crepe paper strips until the bottle is completely covered. Trim any extra crepe paper at the top, if necessary.
3. Paint the bottle cap brown. Set it aside to dry. It will be needed during the Souvenir Pumpkin Pal assembly.
4. Twist or tie a knot at the top of the bottle with the green chenille stick to secure the top of the crepe paper. (Adult assistance is suggested.)
5. Curl the chenille stick ends into vines on either side of the pumpkin. (Adult assistance is suggested.)
6. Glue pumpkin leaves to the pumpkin vine, near the stem (cap).

Souvenir Pumpkin Pal *(cont.)*

My Pumpkin Pal Book

Materials
- *My Pumpkin Pal* book on page 85 or the color version, pumpkin pal.pdf, on the CD
- hole punch

Teacher Preparation
1. Copy and cut out the *My Pumpkin Pal* book pages for each child.
2. Prepare an enlarged color version of the book to share with the class.

Procedure
1. Have children draw their own Pumpkin Pals on page 1 and seeds on page 3.
2. Color the pages of the *My Pumpkin Pal* book.
3. Sequence the pages of the book and staple them together. Do not staple over the hole punch mark.
4. Use the hole punch to punch a hole through the upper left corner of the book pages.

Souvenir Pumpkin Pal Assembly

Materials
- pumpkin projects and completed *My Pumpkin Pal* books
- brown painted caps (See Procedure 3 on page 82.)
- School-Home Connection Ticket: Pumpkin Patch on page 84 for each child
- dry pumpkin seeds

Teacher Preparation
1. Collect the pumpkin projects, books, and caps.
2. Copy and cut out a School-Home Connection Ticket for each child
3. Use a hole punch to punch holes in a corner of each ticket.

Procedure – Stage 1
1. Have each child arrange his or her completed pumpkin project, *My Pumpkin Pal* book, and a brown cap in the work area. Help as needed.
2. Demonstrate how to thread the *My Pumpkin Pal* book through the chenille stick vine on one side. Bend the vine to secure the book. Have children attach their books to their pumpkins.

Procedure – Stage 2
1. Give each child 10 dry pumpkin seeds and ask them to drop them into the pumpkin.
2. Twist the brown cap (pumpkin stem) onto the pumpkin once the seeds are inside.
3. Attach the School-Home Connection Ticket to the other vine on the pumpkin and secure it.
4. Have children take home the Souvenir Pumpkin Pals to share with family and friends.

School-Home Connection

Making the Pumpkin Pal provides each child with a souvenir of the pumpkin patch unit to take home to share what he or she has learned. By sending home this handmade souvenir, along with a copy of the School-Home Connection Ticket, each child will be encouraged to discuss what he or she has learned during the unit. Parents can use the prompts on the ticket as a springboard for discussions, songs, stories, and other activities from the pumpkin patch unit.

Teacher Note: Have an official passport stamping at the end of the pumpkin patch journey.

Souvenir Pumpkin Pal *(cont.)*

School-Home Connection Ticket: Pumpkin Patch

Our class has just finished a study of the pumpkin patch. Each day we learned more about pumpkins. Take a look at your child's Pumpkin Pal souvenir from our "visit" to the pumpkin patch. Find out what he or she learned. You might start by discussing the following:

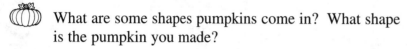

What are some shapes pumpkins come in? What shape is the pumpkin you made?

What colors are pumpkins?

What does a pumpkin need to grow?

What size (color/shape) are pumpkin seeds?

Is a pumpkin a living thing? Is it a plant or an animal? How do you know?

Read aloud the *My Pumpkin Pal* book attached to your child's pumpkin. Encourage your child to complete the directions on the last page after you read the book together.

Pumpkin Leaves Patterns

My Pumpkin Pal **Book**

By:_____

My Pumpkin Pal

My pumpkin is orange, brown, and green.
①

The seeds inside can't be seen.
②

Pour the seeds out and count them.
③

Let's Go to a Winter Wonderland!

Materials

- Winter Wonderland card sets on pages 89–95 or the color versions, wonderland card sets folder, on the CD
- winter-related items (e.g., mittens, paper snowflakes, plastic winter animals)
- winter hat

deer

Teacher Preparation

1. Copy and color a class set of Winter Wonderland card sets, or make color copies of the sets and cut them out.
2. Collect a variety of winter-related items and place them inside the winter hat.

Procedure

1. Have the children sit together in a close group. It is important for all children to be able to see the visual aids and hear the responses from classmates.
2. Introduce the unit on a winter wonderland by presenting the selected visuals, simple questions, and facts about winter.

Where are we going?

Explain to the children that, in their classroom, they will be learning about a winter wonderland. They will be reading about winter, examining winter activities, and learning even more about animals in winter. They will learn new things to help them imagine they are part of a winter wonderland!

Compare and contrast hot and cold weather. Talk about how cold weather affects people, animals, and plants. Ask the children to name things that are hot and others that are cold. Review the seasons and different types of weather (*rainy, cloudy, sunny, windy, snowy*). Ask children what type of weather is their favorite, and why. If appropriate, make a graph to show the results of the discussion.

Read a winter-related book to the children. Use a classroom favorite or choose a new one from the Suggested Books listed on page 87. Show the children the collection of winter-related items inside the winter hat. Ask them what they know about the winter season. Invite children to briefly describe places they have been during the winter season, including some exciting things in nature that they have seen. Help children brainstorm other things they might see during winter. You might wish to start a chart with pictures and labels. Encourage children to add to it for the duration of the journey to a winter wonderland. Incorporate the words from the Winter Wonderland Vocabulary list on page 88 whenever possible. Review the vocabulary words daily with the children.

What is winter?

Display the What Is Winter? card set on the board. Share the following background information about winter:

- Winter is one of four seasons; it is the coldest time of the year.
- Winter sunlight is not as strong as summer sunlight. Less sunlight makes the air, land, and water colder. When water is extremely cold, it freezes.
- Water in clouds can also freeze, making snowflakes. Snowflakes come in different shapes and sizes, but they always have six sides!
- Plants may stop growing. Their leaves may fall off. But the needles on evergreen trees stay green all year!

Let's Go To a Winter Wonderland! *(cont.)*

Procedure *(cont.)*

Who/what will we see in a winter wonderland?

Display the Animals in Winter card set on the board. Talk about animals in winter with the children. Which animals have they seen outside during the winter? (*Deer, birds, squirrels, and other animals may search for food to eat.*)

Briefly discuss where other animals go during the winter. Some animals migrate to warmer parts of the earth where there is more food. (*Monarch butterfly, geese, elk*)

Other animals spend much of the cold winter months in dens. They enter a deep sleep called hibernation. (*grizzly bear, dormouse*) They live off fat they have stored in their bodies. When they come out in spring, these animals are very hungry!

What could we do in a winter wonderland?

Display the What Could We Do? card set on the board. Ask the children to think about activities they like to do during the winter. (*building snow pals, making snow angels, ice fishing, sledding, ice skating, skiing, spending snow days inside, watching snow machines*) If you do not live in an area where it snows, ask the children what kinds of things they would like to do if it snowed in your community.

Review the five senses. Ask children about how they might use each sense when observing a winter wonderland. They might *see* a giant snow pal, *hear* the whoosh of a blast of strong wind, *taste* hot cocoa, *touch* snowflakes with their fingers, and *smell* the scent of hot soup simmering on the stove.

When is the best time to visit a winter wonderland?

Winter in North America lasts from around December 21 to March 21. The months of January and February would be a great time to visit a winter wonderland! **Note:** Winter in the southern hemisphere occurs between June and August.

What type of clothes would you wear?

Talk with the children about cold weather. Have them think about the types of clothes that are necessary to participate in winter activities. Hold up each of the What Should We Wear? card set and ask the children if they think each item would be good to wear in the winter and why. (*A winter hat, mittens, scarf, and snow boots are appropriate winter clothes.*)

Why would you like to visit a winter wonderland?

Invite children to give reasons why they would like to visit a winter wonderland. (*You could see "cool" changes that have occurred due to the arrival of winter: snowflakes, icicles, evergreens with their green needles, and a white blanket of snow.*)

Suggested Books

The First Day of Winter by Denise Fleming

Rabbit's Gift by George Shannon

Snowballs by Lois Ehlert

The Snowman by Raymond Briggs

The Snowy Day by Ezra Jack Keats

Snowmen at Night by Caralyn Buehner

The Tomten and the Fox by Astrid Lindgren

Under My Hood I Have a Hat by Karla Kuskin

When Will It Be Spring? by Catherine Walters

When Winter Comes by Robert Maass

White Snow, Blue Feather by Julie Downing

Winter Is the Warmest Season by Lauren Stringer

Winter Wonderland Vocabulary

Winter Weather

bank	nippy
bare	powder
blanket	shiver
blizzard	shovel
chilly	slippery
crunchy	slope
drift	slushy
evergreens	snowstorm
fluffy	still
frozen	tracks
icicles	wet
icy	white

Snowflakes

blow
crystals
fall
flurry
glisten
hexagon
ice
six-sided
twirl

Snow Machines

icebreaker
snow tires
snowblower
snowplow
tow truck

Winter Activities

ice fishing	snow angel
ice hockey	snow fort
ice skating	snow pal
skiing	snowboarding
sledding	snowman
sleigh ride	snowmobiling
	snowshoeing

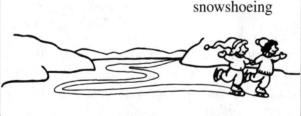

Winter Wear

boots
coat
earmuffs
gloves
hat
mittens
parka
scarf
snow pants
snowsuit
sweater
wool socks

Winter Information – What Animals Do in the Winter

Migrate	Hibernate	Stay Active
geese	bat	beaver
elk	bear	deer
Monarch butterfly	chipmunk	fox
whale	frog	mouse
	groundhog	rabbit
	insect	squirrel
	skunk	weasel
	snake	

Winter Wonderland—What Is Winter? Cards

snowflakes

evergreen tree

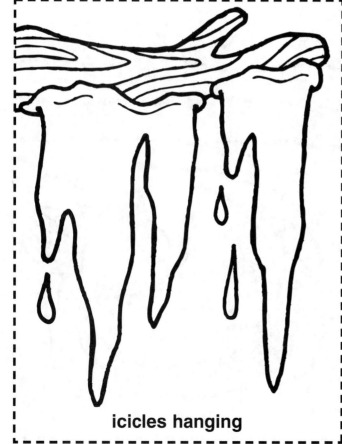

icicles hanging

animal tracks in the snow

Winter Wonderland—Animals in Winter Cards

deer   rabbit

junco   dormouse

Winter Wonderland—Animals in Winter Cards *(cont.)*

fox

squirrel

beaver

weasel

Winter Wonderland – What Could We Do? Cards

Winter Wonderland – What Could We Do? Cards *(cont.)*

Winter Wonderland – What Could We Do? Cards *(cont.)*

Winter Wonderland – What Should We Wear? Cards

"Snow Is Falling!"

Readiness Standards

Reading
- understands that illustrations and pictures convey meaning
- knows that words are made up of syllables (i.e., syllables are blended to form words)
- retells a story with attention to the sequence of main events
- uses new vocabulary to describe experiences and observations

Materials

- "Snow Is Falling!" rhyming story poster pages 98–99 or the color version, snow story.pdf, on the CD
- "Snow Is Falling!" Animals on pages 100–101 or the color version, snow animals.pdf, on the CD
- "Snow Is Falling!" Winter Habitats on pages 102–105 or the color version, winter habitats.pdf, on the CD
- hole punch
- Velcro® (adhesive hook and loop)

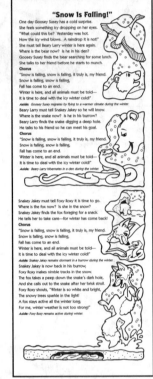

Teacher Preparation

1. Copy, color, cut out, and laminate the animals or make color copies.

2. Attach the hook side of the Velcro® to the back of each animal card. Place the Velcro so the animal will fit properly in his habitat.

3. Copy, color, cut out, and laminate the Winter Habitats or make color copies.

4. Attach the loop side of the Velcro to each Winter Habitat card where indicated.

5. Display the Winter Habitat cards in the room for all to view.

6. Plan to spend a few days immersing children in this rhyming variation of the Chicken Little story. You may wish to share the original version, first to remind children of the story.

7. Read the rhyming story, "Snow Is Falling!" to the children. The more you read the story, the more familiar they will be with it, and the more they will be able to participate.

   - **Preview** new vocabulary, such as *migrates, hibernates, den, remains dormant, burrow, foraging, nimble, brisk, stroll,* and *sly,* with the children.
   - **Note** the different pairs of rhyming words.
   - **Discuss/Practice** the chorus and the refrains:
     "Snow is falling, snow is falling, it truly is, my friend ..."
     "Where is the ...? Is she/he in his/her ...?"

"Snow Is Falling!" *(cont.)*

Procedure

1. Explain to the children that you will be sharing a variation of "Chicken Little" called "Snow Is Falling!" and that the new story rhymes. Read "Snow Is Falling!" to the group. Introduce the habitat cards. Ask which animal might live in each one.

2. Distribute the animal cards to selected children. Ask them to look at their cards and note what the animal in the card is doing. Explain that when the animal doing that specific action is mentioned in the story, the child is to stand and hold up the card as long as that animal is a part of the story.

3. Again read the "Snow Is Falling!" rhyming story to the group. This time, invite children to participate by standing up when his or her animal (and action) is featured.

4. When an animal in the story goes to its winter habitat, have the child give his or her card to a classmate (without a card) to attach it to the correct winter habitat.

5. Continue in this manner for the remainder of the rhyming story. Repeat it often until children can tell the story themselves.

Revisiting the Rhyming Story

Once children are familiar with "Snow Is Falling!" try the following activities:

1. Share several two-syllable words from the rhyming story by segmenting them. Then have the children repeat the entire word with you (*win-ter, tru-ly, ic-y, ac-tive, wea-ther, sur-prise, fall-ing, a-gain, bur-row*).

2. Have the children retell the main events of the story. If necessary, use the animal and habitat cards to help them recall the correct sequence of events.

> Goosey Susey notices a snowflake.
>
> Goosey Susey warns Beary Larry about winter weather.
>
> Goosey Susey *migrates* to a warmer place.
>
> Beary Larry warns Snakey Jakey.
>
> Beary Larry *hibernates* in a den.
>
> Snakey Jakey warns Foxy Roxy.
>
> Snakey Jakey *remains dormant* in a burrow.
>
> Foxy Roxy *stays active* during the winter.

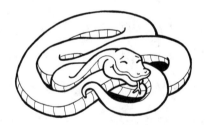

3. Discuss the action of each animal during the winter season.
   migrate—Goosey Susey flies south to warmer weather.
   hibernate—Beary Larry sleeps in a den.
   dormant—Snakey Jakey remains still in a burrow.
   active—Foxy Roxy stays active in the snowy cold.

Character Concept

Even though it's time for Goosey Susey to migrate for the winter, she stops to take time to warn her friend. Beary Larry then warns another friend, and so on. How do you feel when someone helps you? Ask the children, "Can you think of a time when a friend warned you to keep you safe?" Invite the children to share their experiences with the class.

"Snow Is Falling!"

One day Goosey Susey has a cold surprise.

She feels something icy dropping on her eyes.

"What could this be? Yesterday was hot.

Now the icy wind blows. A raindrop it is not!"

She must tell Beary Larry winter is here again.

Where is the bear now? Is he in his den?

Goosey Susey finds the bear searching for some lunch.

She talks to her friend before he starts to munch.

Chorus

"Snow is falling, snow is falling, it truly is, my friend.

Snow is falling, snow is falling,

Fall has come to an end.

Winter is here, and all animals must be told—

It is time to deal with the icy winter cold!"

Aside: *Goosey Susey migrates by flying to a warmer climate during the winter.*

Beary Larry must tell Snakey Jakey so he will know.

Where is the snake now? Is he in his burrow?

Beary Larry finds the snake digging a deep hole.

He talks to his friend so he can meet his goal.

Chorus

"Snow is falling, snow is falling, it truly is, my friend.

Snow is falling, snow is falling,

Fall has come to an end.

Winter is here, and all animals must be told—

It is time to deal with the icy winter cold!"

Aside: *Beary Larry hibernates in a den during the winter.*

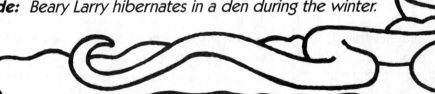

Snakey Jakey must tell Foxy Roxy it is time to go.

Where is the fox now? Is she in the snow?

Snakey Jakey finds the fox foraging for a snack.

He tells her to take care—for winter has come back!

Chorus

"Snow is falling, snow is falling, it truly is, my friend.

Snow is falling, snow is falling,

Fall has come to an end.

Winter is here, and all animals must be told—

It is time to deal with the icy winter cold!"

Aside: *Snakey Jakey remains dormant in a burrow during the winter.*

Snakey Jakey is now back in his burrow,

Foxy Roxy makes nimble tracks in the snow.

The fox takes a peep down the snake's dark hole,

And she calls out to the snake after her brisk stroll.

Foxy Roxy shouts, "Winter is so white and bright,

The snowy trees sparkle in the light!

A fox stays active all the winter long;

For me, winter weather is not too strong!"

Aside: *Foxy Roxy remains active during winter.*

"Snow Is Falling!" Animals

"Snow Is Falling!" Animals *(cont.)*

"Snow Is Falling!" Winter Habitats

"Snow Is Falling!" Winter Habitats *(cont.)*

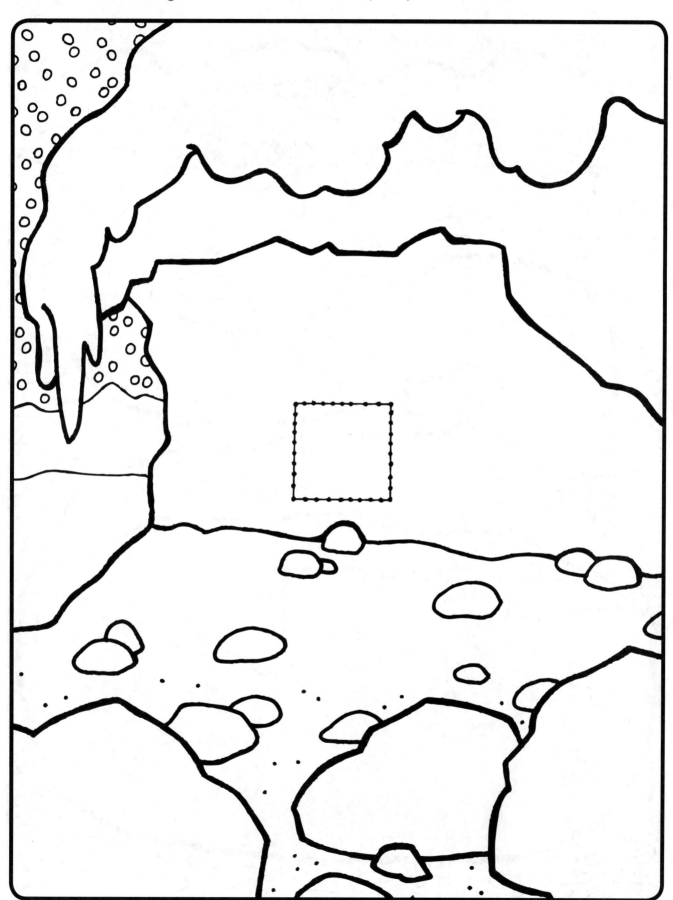

"Snow Is Falling!" Winter Habitats *(cont.)*

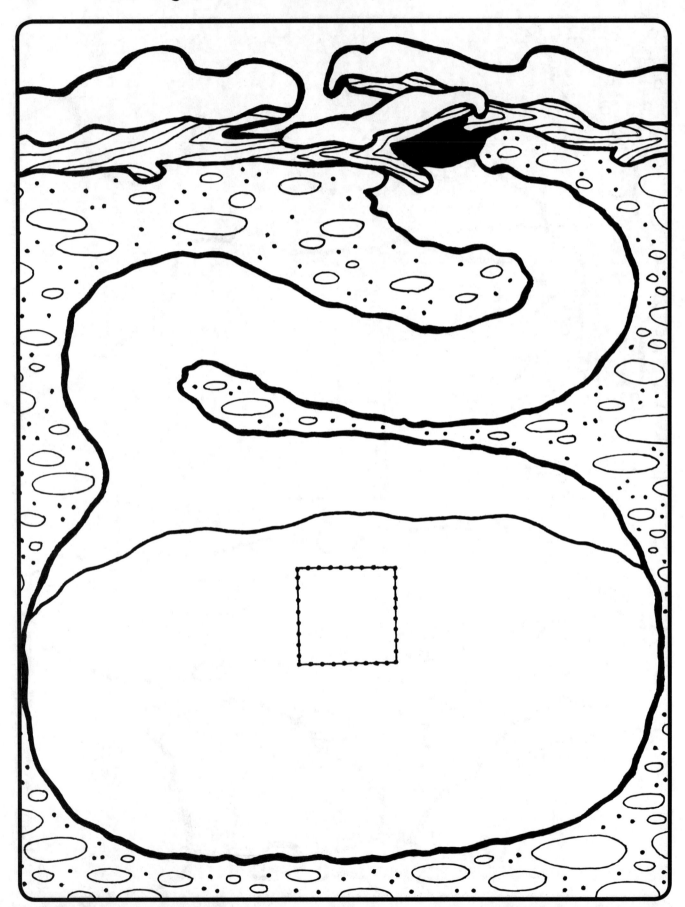

"Snow Is Falling!" Winter Habitats *(cont.)*

Writing in the Snow

── Readiness Standards ──

Writing
- uses knowledge of letters to write or copy familiar words, such as names
- uses drawings to express thoughts, feelings, and ideas

Fine Motor
- works with a variety of textures and materials

Materials
- shaving cream (non-mentholated)
- shallow tray or flat surface
- cardstock

Teacher Preparation
1. Spray shaving cream on a shallow tray.
2. Print each child's name on a small piece of cardstock.
3. Place the tray and name cards on a table at a center.

Procedure
1. Invite children to take turns printing (finger-writing) their names in the shaving cream (snow). Encourage them to use their name cards for reference if necessary.
2. Next, ask each child to draw a winter item or scene in the "snow."

Winter Whites

── Readiness Standards ──

Fine Motor
- practices tactile discrimination
- counts objects

Math
- knows that numbers are used in real-world situations

Materials
- white sequins or snowflake confetti
- white Styrofoam® packing peanuts
- water table or sand table
- number cards (optional)
- white pom-poms
- cotton balls
- 4 white socks

Teacher Preparation
1. Fill a water table with white Styrofoam® packing peanuts.
2. Mix in the sequins, pom-poms, and cotton balls with the packing peanuts.
3. Hide the white socks deep in the mixture.
4. If appropriate, prepare number cards for each item you wish children to find and count.

Procedure
1. Share with the children that two little children have lost their socks in a blizzard. How many socks do they need to find? (*four*)
2. Have each child take a turn searching through the "snow" to find the four socks.
3. Challenge the child to find specific numbers of other winter items (e.g., 3 cotton balls [*soft snow*], 5 pom-poms [*snowballs*], 2 sequins [*snowflakes*]).

Snowflake Pairs

Readiness Standards

Reading
- uses visual discrimination skills

Math
- groups objects by attributes (e.g., shape)

Social Skills
- takes turns
- cooperates with others

Materials
- Ice Skates Patterns on page 108 or the color versions, ice skates.pdf, on the CD
- Snowflake Cards on page 109 or the color versions, snowflakes.pdf, on the CD
- metal cookie sheet or cardboard
- adhesive magnets
- white cardstock
- aluminum foil (optional)

Teacher Preparation
1. Copy, color, and cut out the Ice Skates Patterns or make color copies.
2. Make two copies of the Snowflake Cards on white cardstock and cut them out.
3. Attach an adhesive magnet to the back of each skate and snowflake.
4. If desired, wrap aluminum foil around the cookie sheet to create a skating rink.
   Note: If you are not making a magnetic game, cover a piece of cardboard with aluminum foil to create a skating rink.
5. Attach the ice skates to the cookie sheet and place the snowflake cards on the table.

Procedure
1. Children will work in pairs, spreading the Snowflake Cards face up on a table.
2. The first child chooses a snowflake and places it on an ice skate.
3. The partner carefully looks at the snowflake on the ice skate and selects the matching one from the remaining snowflake cards.
4. He or she then places the snowflake on the other ice skate.
5. The snowflakes are removed from the ice skates and set in a "snow pile."
6. The second child chooses a snowflake and places it on an ice skate.
7. The partner selects the match and places it on the other ice skate.
8. The snowflakes are removed from the ice skates and set in the snow pile.
9. The game continues in this manner until all snowflakes have been matched.

Ice Skates Patterns

Snowflake Cards

"Melting Snow Pal"

Readiness Standards

Fine Motor

- cuts and pastes

Science

- understands simple cause-and-effect relationships
- develops predictions based on previous experiences

Materials

- "Melting Snow Pal" poems on page 111 or the color versions, melting snow pals.pdf, on the CD
- Snow Pal Scarf, Hat, and Sun Patterns on page 111
- sheet of white construction paper for each child
- candy corn or orange paper scraps
- 2 wiggle eyes for each child
- 2 small twigs for each child
- yellow construction paper
- colorful-patterned paper
- plastic knife and spoons

- felt (variety of colors)
- crystal-colored glitter
- crayons and markers
- white tempera paint
- permanent marker
- pitcher of water
- metal pie dish
- safety scissors
- white glue
- cardstock

Teacher Preparation

1. Copy the Scarf, Hat, and Sun Patterns onto cardstock and cut them out.
2. Copy and cut out a "Melting Snow Pal" poem for each child or make color copies.
3. Use a permanent marker to trace the hat pattern onto colored felt. Make a hat for each child.
4. Trace one sun pattern onto yellow construction paper for each child. Trace the scarf onto colored paper. Precut these pieces if necessary.
5. In a pie dish, make a mixture of 2-parts white tempera paint, 1-part white glue, and 1-part water for each child. Stir crystal-colored glitter into the mixture with a plastic spoon.
6. Using a plastic knife, cut the orange wedge from a candy corn for each child.

Procedure

1. Read the "Melting Snow Pal" poem to the group. Ask the children if they have ever built a snow pal. Discuss what happened when the weather got warmer. (*When the sun came out, it melted.*)
2. Tell the children that they will be doing an art project to show what happens to a snow pal when the sun comes out! Give each child a sheet of construction paper to fold "hamburger style."
3. Have each child draw a snowman on the left side of the paper. Glue the poem to the top of the right side of the paper.
4. Provide scissors for each child to cut out a Sun pattern and to cut a strip of colored paper to make a scarf. Assist as needed.
5. Pour a small amount of the paint mixture onto the bottom right side of the white paper (under the poem) to make the body for the melted snow pal.
6. Add twigs, wiggle eyes, a candy corn nose, a felt hat, and a colorful scarf to the mixture to complete the melted snow pal.

"Melting Snow Pal" Poems

Scarf, Hat, and Sun Patterns

Note: *He* and *she* options are provided for the poem.

"Melting Snow Pal"

One little snow pal,
Sitting in the sun.
He melted away,
Then there was none!

Why did the snow pal melt?

"Melting Snow Pal"

One little snow pal,
Sitting in the sun.
She melted away,
Then there was none!

Why did the snow pal melt?

Ice Sculpture

─ Readiness Standards ─

Science

- knows that the physical properties of things can change
- uses the senses (sight, touch) to make observations about nonliving objects

Fine Motor

- uses pincer grasp to manipulate eyedroppers and tongs

Materials

- access to water and a freezer
- small recyclable containers
- large recyclable containers
- plastic eyedroppers
- food coloring
- water table
- rock salt

Teacher Preparation

1. Fill the large containers with water and freeze them.
2. Remove the ice from the containers and place the ice in a water table. (If the ice does not slide easily from the plastic containers, hold the container under warm water until it does.)
3. In each small container, make colored water using water and food coloring.
4. Place the containers of colored water, rock salt, and plastic eyedroppers at the water table.

Procedure

1. Have the children sprinkle handfuls of rock salt onto the ice forms.
2. Direct the children to watch carefully as the ice changes and cavities form.
3. Have the children use plastic eyedroppers to drop colored water into the cavities.
4. Continue to observe the changes as the ice melts.

Ice Sculpture Extension

Additional Materials

- 1" tissue-paper squares (variety of colors)
- tongs
- plastic plates

Teacher Preparation

Place different-colored 1" tissue-paper squares on plates near the ice sculpture activity as it comes to an end.

Procedure

1. Invite children to use tongs to carry the remaining ice to the plates, and lay the ice on the paper squares.
2. Use the tongs to move the ice around on top of the paper squares.
3. Observe the colors that bleed together and the beautiful color combinations that emerge.

Giant Bear Den

Readiness Standards

Fine Motor
- paints on a variety of textures, from under and above an object

Gross Motor
- crawls

Cognitive Skills
- uses imagination (i.e., pretends to be a bear)

Materials
- large appliance box and several smaller appliance boxes (with brown interiors)
- small bowls or containers for paint
- smock or old shirt for each child
- craft knife (for adult use only)
- gray and brown paint
- old newspapers
- paintbrushes
- duct tape
- paint, a variety of colors (optional)
- leaves and branches (optional)

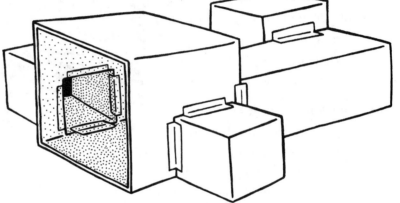

Teacher Preparation
1. Build a mock den from the boxes. Use the large appliance box as the main portion of the den and the smaller boxes for alcoves and tunnels.
2. Use the craft knife and duct tape to connect the boxes to each other. Do this prior to the children's arrival. **Warning:** Children should never use the craft knife.
3. Lay down old newspapers to cover the floor under and around the assembled den.
4. Pour gray and brown paint into the bowls and arrange the bowls on the newspaper around the den.

Procedure
1. This will be an exciting but messy activity! Begin by sharing a book about bears in dens. If you do not have one in your library, try *When Will It Be Spring?* by Catherine Walters.
2. Give each child a smock and a paintbrush and explain that they will be painting the boxes to look like a bear den out in the woods. Ask them, "What is a den made of? What colors might it be?"
3. Have children paint the inside of the largest box first. (The other attached box interiors can stay brown like dirt.)
4. Let the paint dry. The next day, paint the outside of the den using the brown and gray paint. If you wish, add green to suggest leaves or attach real leaves and branches.
5. If desired, provide different colored paints and allow children to add gems and minerals to the den walls.
6. Allow your little classroom bears to use this den to pretend to hibernate!

Triangle Evergreen Trees
── Readiness Standards ──

Math
- knows that geometric shapes can be put together to form other shapes
- sorts objects by size

Fine Motor
- paints with a variety of implements

Materials
- white or silver sequins
- crystal-colored glitter
- brown ink stamp pads
- green tempera paint
- shallow dishes
- large sponges
- white paper
- newspaper (optional)

Teacher Preparation
1. Create three different-sized triangular sponge stamps (*small, medium, large*). When stacked on top of each other, they should fit on the paper.
2. Pour green tempera paint into shallow dishes.
3. Place the triangular sponge stamps, dishes of paint, sequins, glitter, stamp pads, and white paper on a table or at a center.

Procedure
1. Discuss winter trees with children. Explain that some trees, called evergreens, have needles instead of leaves. Explain that they do not lose all their needles at the same time in winter, so they remain green.
2. Show children the three different-sized sponges and discuss them. Which sponge would be the base of the tree (*large triangle*), which would work for the middle (*medium-sized triangle*), and which would make the best top (*smallest triangle*)? What else does the tree need? (*a trunk*)
3. Invite children to create trees. First, make a trunk on a piece of white paper. To do this, stamp his or her pinky in the brown-ink stamp pad and print it at the bottom of the white paper.
4. Then dip the largest triangle sponge into green paint. Stamp the sponge above the brown stem to create the bottom portion of an evergreen tree.
5. Dip the medium sponge into green paint and stamp it above the large green triangle.
6. Dip the smallest sponge in green paint and stamp it above the medium green triangle to create the top portion of the evergreen tree.
7. Have children wash and dry their hands and then add sequins and glitter to the wet green evergreen to create snowflakes on the tree.

Jack Frost Movement Game

Readiness Standards

Gross Motor	Social	Fine Motor
• dances to music	• follows the rules of a game • takes turns	• cuts • pastes

Jack Frost Movement Game

Materials
- Jack Frost's Hat (See directions on page 116.)
- Jack Frost's Snow Wand (See directions below.)
- Snowflake Necklace for each child (See directions on page 116.)
- gentle music such as Vivaldi's *Four Seasons,* "Winter" or George Winstons's *Winter*

Teacher Preparation
1. Gather Jack Frost's Hat and Snow Wand, and distribute a Snowflake Necklace to each child.
2. Set up the gentle music.

Note: Each child will be able to make a snowflake necklace for this activity. Some of these children may also help make the hat and wand.

Procedure
1. Invite children to take turns being Jack Frost by wearing Jack Frost's Hat and holding the Snow Wand.
2. Have the other children wear the snowflake necklaces and spread out around the room.
3. As the music plays, Jack Frost will move quietly, lightly touching each snowflake with the wand.
4. When touched, each snowflake will come to life and dance. When the music stops, each snowflake should gently fall to the floor.
5. Allow another child to play Jack Frost and continue in the same manner.

Jack Frost's Snow Wand

Materials
- Star Patterns on page 118
- white and silver ribbons
- dowel, about 12" long
- silver glitter and glue

Teacher Preparation
Make a copy of the Star Patterns and cut out two stars.

Procedure
1. Have two children spread glue on the stars and sprinkle silver glitter on them.
2. Glue white and silver ribbon streamers to the backs of the stars.
3. Glue the two stars back-to-back around the top of the dowel to create Jack Frost's Snow Wand.

Jack Frost Movement Game *(cont.)*

Jack Frost's Hat

Materials

- Icicle Patterns on page 117 or the color versions, icicles.pdf, on the CD
- 9" x 12" sheet of white construction paper
- six 6" lengths of white string or yarn
- silver glitter and glue
- tape

Teacher Preparation

1. Copy and cut out the Icicle Patterns or make color copies.
2. Cut one large half circle (9" diameter) from the white construction paper and roll it into a cone shape as shown. **Note:** Make the hat opening a bit larger than the top of a child's head.
3. Tape the cone closed. Trim off any excess at the bottom.

Procedure

1. Tape one end of each 6" string to an icicle pattern. Have a few of the children add glitter to the icicles. Use tape to attach the other end of the icicle strings inside the bottom edges of the sides and back of the hat.
2. Add glitter to the snowflake pattern and glue it to the front of the hat to complete Jack Frost's Hat.

Snowflake Necklace

Materials

- 24" lengths of white string or yarn for each child
- heavy white paper or cardstock
- snowflake pattern (on the right)
- hole punch and scissors
- glitter and glue
- white or blue plastic beads

Teacher Preparation

1. Copy the snowflake pattern on heavy paper for each child. If necessary, help children cut out the patterns.
2. Arrange areas where children can work gluing glitter and stringing beads.

Procedure

1. Give each child a snowflake to cut around and yarn or string to finish the necklace.
2. Help each child punch a hole in the snowflake and attach a string to the snowflake to create a necklace. **Note:** Do not close the necklaces if beads will be added.
3. Invite children to add glitter to their necklaces.
4. If adding beads, wrap tape around the ends of the string to create needles to ease the beads onto the strings.

Jack Frost Movement Game *(cont.)*

Icicle Patterns

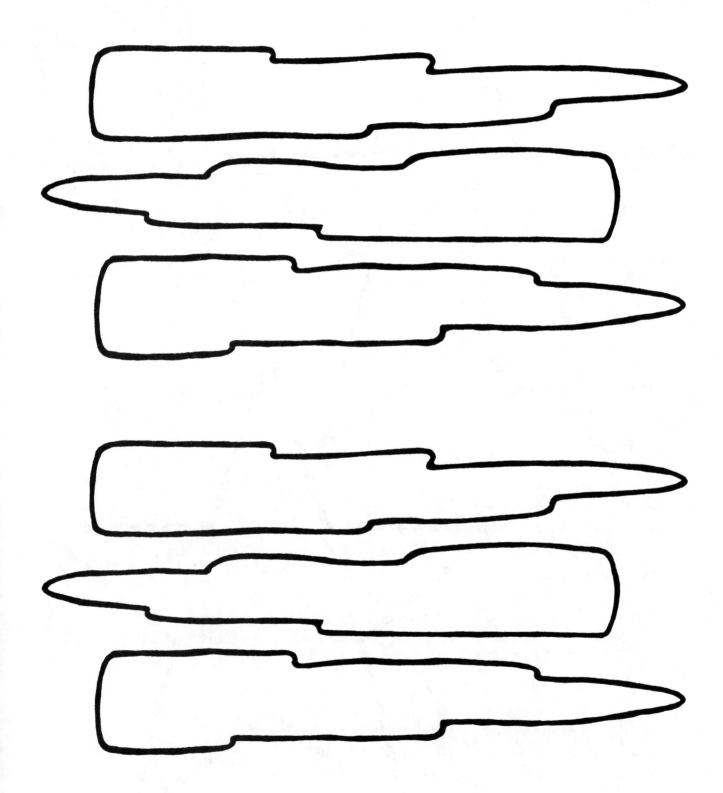

Jack Frost Movement Game *(cont.)*

Star Patterns

Snowball Drop

Readiness Standards

Fine Motor	Social	Gross Motor
• scoops and balances • practices eye-hand coordination	• cooperates with others • shares with others	• runs

Materials

- large container for each team
- small container for each team
- large spoon or ladle for each team
- masking tape
- cotton balls or Ping-Pong balls

Teacher Preparation

1. Mark a starting line and a finish line on the floor using masking tape.
2. Put cotton balls into each small container and place the containers at the starting line.
3. Place the larger containers at the finish line.
4. Create teams of three or more members.

Procedure

1. Explain to children that they will have a relay game and imagine that the cotton balls are snowballs. They will work together in teams.
2. Each child will take a turn carrying a snowball on a spoon from the team's small container at the starting line to the team's larger container at the finish line.
3. He or she will then run back to the starting line and hand the spoon to the next teammate.
4. Continue until each team member has carried a snowball and run back.

Bundle Up!

Readiness Standards

Math	Self-Help	Social
• understands one-to-one correspondence	• puts on and takes off clothing	• works together as part of a group

Materials

- winter hats, earmuffs, mittens, scarves, jackets

Teacher Preparation

1. Divide the class into two or three teams.
2. Gather the materials and place each team's clothing in a separate pile.
3. Ensure you have at least one similar item of clothing for each child on a team.

Procedure

1. When you give the signal to begin, both teams race to put on the clothes.
2. Each child puts on just one item of winter clothing.
3. The winning team is the one that finishes dressing first.

"I Built a Snowman!" Fingerplay

Readiness Standards

Listening Skills
- acts out familiar rhymes
- listens for a variety of reasons (e.g., for enjoyment)

Motor Skills
- performs finger movements
- practice gross-motor movements

Materials
- "I Built a Little Snowman!" Cards and Patterns on pages 121–123 or the color versions, I built a snowman.pdf, on the CD
- magnetic surface (e.g., board, cookie sheet)
- adhesive magnets
- markers

Teacher Preparation
1. Copy, color, and cut out the "I Built a Little Snowman!" Cards and Patterns or make color copies.
2. Attach a magnet to each snowman card and pattern.

Procedure
1. Share the "I Built a Little Snowman!" poem by posting the card on a magnetic surface and reading it aloud to the children.

2. Reread the poem, demonstrating how to perform the movements as indicated. Invite the children to perform the movements as you share the poem once more.

3. Attach the Little Snowman pattern to the magnetic surface.

4. Read the poem again. Pause after reading the second line of the poem. Direct a child to add the carrot nose pattern to the snowman's face after the second line.

5. Continue reading the poem. Pause just before reading the last line of the poem. Invite another child to remove the snowman's nose, then finish reading the poem.

6. Repeat steps 1–5 for the variations, "I Built a Tall Snowman" and "I Built a Plump Snowman" by posting the corresponding card and pattern, and adding and removing the popcorn hat and then the raisin eyes.

Along came a deer.

"I Built a Little Snowman!"

Author Unknown

I built a little snowman.
(Make small circle with hands.)

He had a carrot nose.
(Point to nose.)

Along came a bunny.
(Hold up first two fingers, slightly bent.)

And what do you suppose?

That hungry little bunny,
(Make bunny again.)

Looking for his lunch,
(Hop bunny around.)

Ate the snowman's nose.
(Pretend bunny is eating nose.)
(Remove carrot from snowman.)

Nibble! Nibble! Crunch!
(Pretend to be eating a carrot.)

Little Snowman Patterns

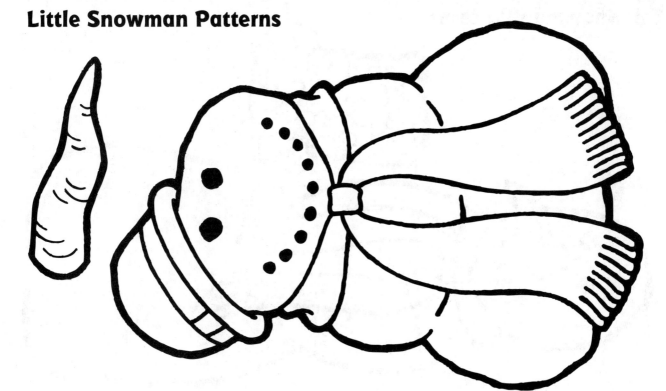

"I Built a Tall Snowman!"

I built a tall snowman.
(Make tall circle with hands.)

He had a popcorn hat.
(Point to head.)

Along came a deer.
(Pretend to be a deer.)

And what do you think of that?

That hungry little deer,
(Pretend to be a deer sniffing the air.)

Looking for a snack,
(Prance like a deer.)

Ate the snowman's hat.
(Pretend deer is eating hat.)
(Remove hat from snowman.)

Nibble! Nibble! Smack!
(Pretend to be eating popcorn.)

Tall Snowman Patterns

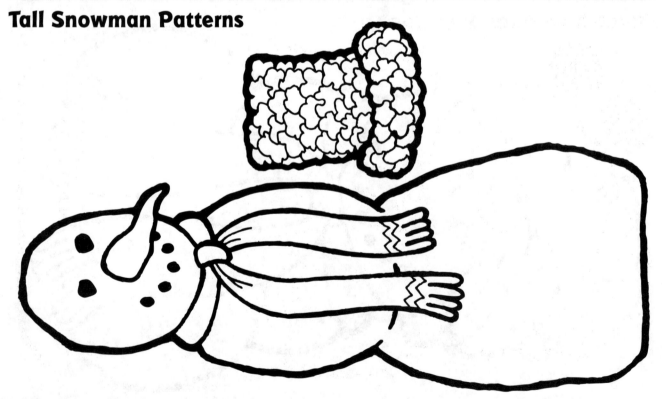

"I Built a Plump Snowman!"

I built a plump snowman.
(Make large circle with hands.)

He had two raisin eyes.
(Point to eyes.)

Along came a bird.
(Flap arms like wings of bird.)

And, oh what a surprise!

That hungry little bird,
(Pretend to be bird pecking about.)

Looking for food to slurp,
(Flap arms like wings of bird.)

Ate the snowman's eyes.
(Pretend bird is nibbling the eyes.)
(Remove raisins from snowman.)

Nibble! Nibble! Burp!
(Pretend to be eating raisins.)

Plump Snowman Patterns

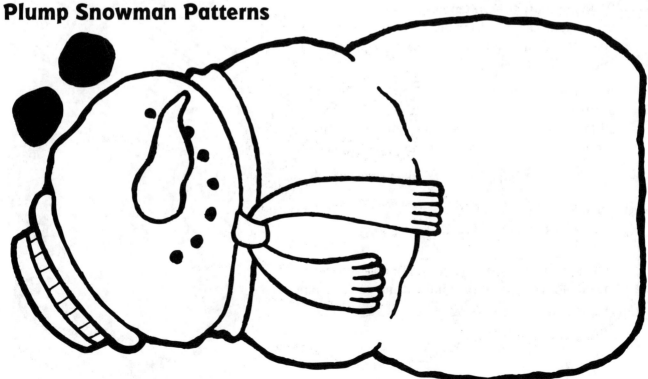

Souvenir Memory Mittens

This is the culminating activity for the winter unit—the take-home souvenir! Assembling this project requires some prep time, depending on the students' cutting abilities. Adult assistance can be helpful and will also provide children with more opportunities to share what they have learned about winter while working on the project. It is suggested that the mittens be assembled one day and the animal and activity cards on another day.

Mittens

Materials

- Mitten Patterns on pages 126–127 or color versions, mittens.pdf, on the CD
- $\frac{1}{4}$" wide ribbon, two 30" lengths for each child (variety of colors)
- 4 sheets of white cardstock for each child
- packing tape
- hole punch
- glitter glue

Teacher Preparation

1. Copy the Souvenir Memory Mitten Patterns onto white cardstock. Each child will need one Activities Mitten and a blank back and one Animals Mitten and a blank back. You will need a total of four mitten patterns.

2. Trace the mitten patterns onto cardstock and cut them out.

3. Place the Activities Mitten Pattern and its matching mitten (back) pattern together. Punch holes as indicated around the perimeter of the mitten using a hole punch.

4. Attach a piece of tape to the end of a 30" length of ribbon to form a "needle." Thread the ribbon all the way through a bottom hole and secure the end to the back of the mitten using packing tape.

5. Follow steps 3 and 4 for the Animals Mitten Pattern.

Procedure

1. Lace the ribbon through each mitten to create a stitching pattern. (Assist students as needed.)

2. When finished, cut off the excess ribbon and secure the end to the back of the mitten using packing tape.

3. Decorate the mittens using glitter glue as desired. Set them aside to dry.

Souvenir Memory Mittens *(cont.)*

Winter Cards

Materials
- Winter Animal Cards on page 128 or the color versions, winter animals.pdf, on the CD
- Winter Activity Cards on page 129 or the color versions, winter activities.pdf, on the CD
- markers or crayons

Teacher Preparation
1. Copy the Winter Animal Cards for each child or make color copies.
2. Copy the Winter Activity Cards for each child or make color copies.

Procedure
1. Color and cut out the Winter Animal Cards.
2. Color and cut out the Winter Activity Cards.

Souvenir Memory Mittens Assembly

Materials
- Mittens for each child
- Animal Cards for each child
- Activity Cards for each child
- $\frac{1}{4}$" wide ribbon
- stapler
- hole punch
- School-Home Connection Ticket: Winter Wonderland on page 129 for each child

Teacher Preparation
1. Copy the School-Home Connection Ticket for each child.
2. Cut a 6" length of ribbon for each child.
3. Gather the ribbon, completed mittens, and Animal and Activity Cards for each child.

Procedure
1. Sort the cards into two piles: one for animals in winter and one for winter activities.
2. Slip the Winter Animal Cards into the Animals Mitten. Slip the Winter Activity Cards into the Activities Mitten.
3. Punch a hole in the Winter Wonderland ticket and slide it to the middle of the 6" ribbon before connecting the mittens.
4. Connect the two completed mittens as shown by stapling the ends of the ribbon to each mitten.
5. Have children take home the Souvenir Memory Mittens to share with family and friends.

School-Home Connection: Winter Wonderland

Making the Memory Mittens provides each child with a souvenir of the winter wonderland unit to take home to share what he or she has learned. By sending home this homemade souvenir, along with a copy of the School-Home Connection Ticket, each child will be encouraged to discuss what he or she has learned during the unit. Parents can use the prompts on the ticket as a springboard for discussions, songs, stories, and other activities from the winter wonderland unit.

Note: Don't forget to have an official passport stamping at the end of the winter journey.

Mitten Pattern—Activities

left

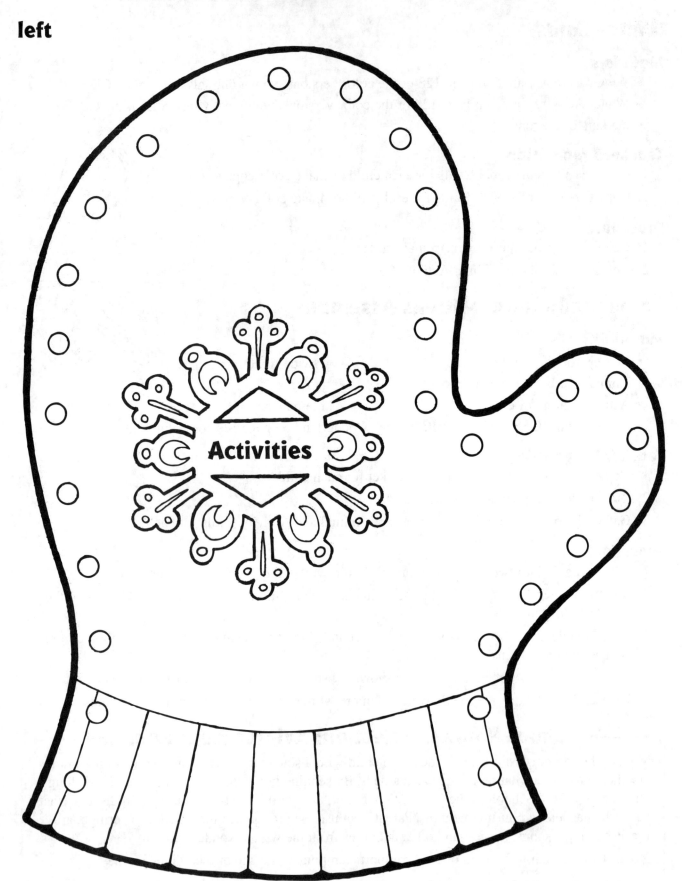

Mitten Pattern—Animals

right

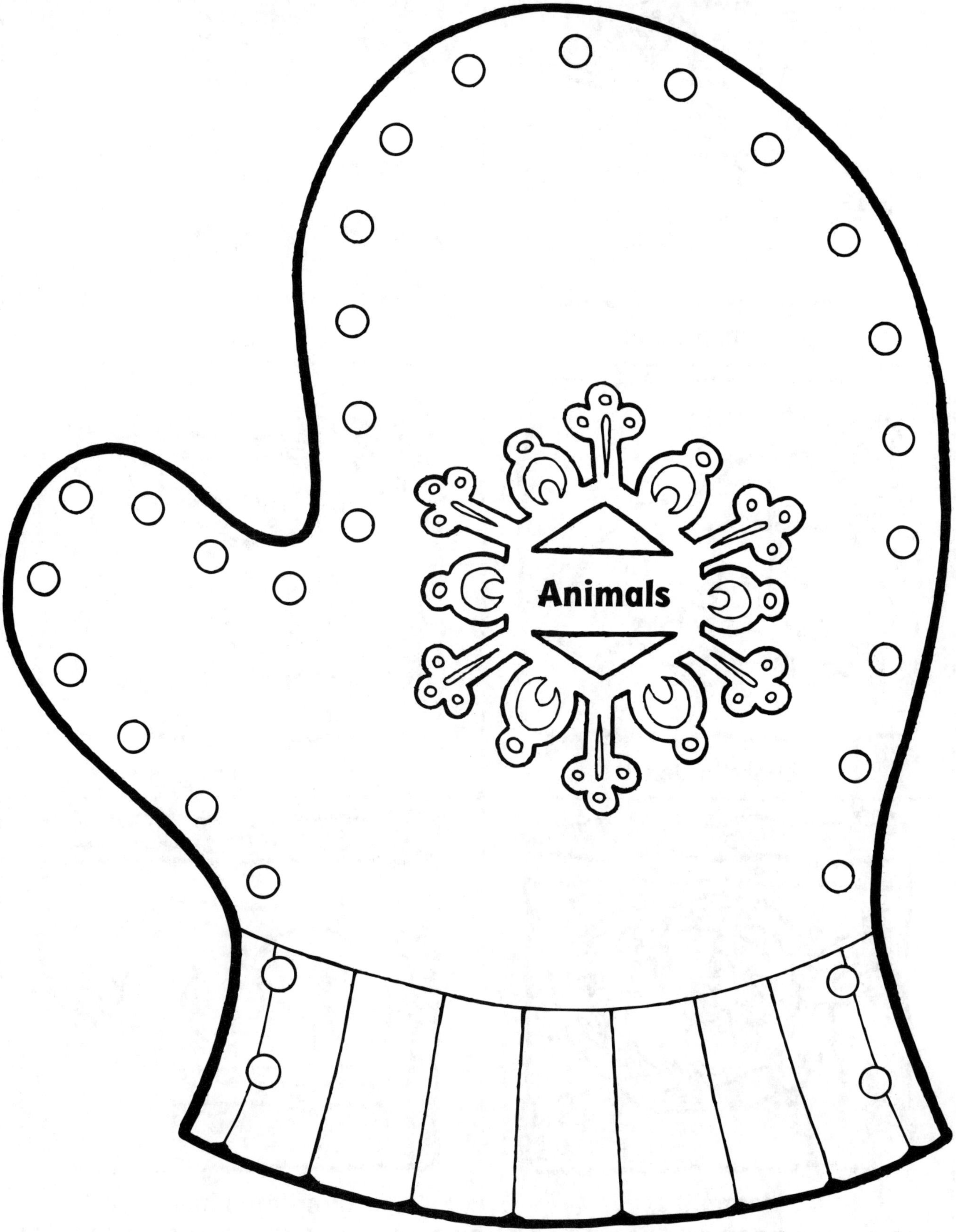

Animals

Winter Animal Cards

geese migrating

rabbit

bears in den

deer

dormouse

groundhogs in burrow

Winter Activity Cards

snow pal

sled

skis

ice skates

School-Home Connection Ticket: Winter Wonderland

Our class has just finished a study of winter. Each day we learned more about the season. Look at your child's Memory Mittens souvenir from our "visit" to a winter wonderland. Find out what he or she learned. You might start by discussing the following:

❋ Why do we wear coats (hats/boots/mittens) in the winter?

❋ What activities can you do in the snow?

❋ What do animals do in winter? (hibernate/migrate/stay active)

❋ Create an imaginary snow pal. Would it be a person or an animal?
Describe what it would look like. What materials would you need to build it?

Let's Go to the Pond!

Materials
- pond-related items (e.g., plastic frogs and insects, foam lily pad, fish-shaped crackers)
- Pond Patterns on pages 133–137 or the color versions, pond patterns.pdf, on the CD
- blue bulletin board paper or poster board
- pail

Teacher Preparation

1. Copy and color a class set of Pond Patterns, or make color copies and cut them out.

2. Cut out a large pond shape using the blue bulletin board paper to fit on a flannel or magnetic board. One long side of the pattern should be flat. When used, the flat side will be at the top to suggest the top of the water in the pond. The pond, when placed on the board, will be viewed as a cross section showing which animals inhabit the water above the waterline and which animals live under water.

3. Put a variety of pond-related items (e.g., a plastic frog, a foam lily pad, fish-shaped crackers, rubber snake) in a pail.

Procedure

1. Have the children sit together in a close group for circle time or whole-group time. It is important for all children to be able to see the visual aids and hear the responses from classmates.

2. Introduce the unit on pond life by presenting the selected visuals, simple questions, and facts.

Where are we going?

Explain to children that, in their classroom, they will be learning about ponds. They will be reading about pond life, examining the parts of a pond, and learning even more about pond plants and animals. They will learn many new things that will help them imagine they are part of a real pond!

Read a pond-themed book to the children. Use a classroom favorite or choose a new one from the Suggested Books listed on page 131. Share the collection of pond-related items in the pail. Ask children where they think these things are found. Ask them what they know about ponds. *A pond is an area of fresh, still water that can be any shape or size. It can be man-made or natural.* Invite children who have visited a pond to briefly describe their experiences. Explain that they will be learning more about ponds.

Who/what will we see at the pond?

Ask children what they might see at a pond. *They might see beavers, frogs, ducks, dragonflies, fish, and other animals that live on, in, or near the pond. They might also see pond plants, such as water lilies, duckweed, and cattails.* Display the large pond cutout on a flannel or magnetic board. Begin by attaching the Above the Pond Patterns (page 133) to the scene. Proceed by attaching the Near the Pond (page 134), Top of the Pond (page 135), In the Pond (page 136), and Bottom of the Pond Patterns (page 137), one level at a time. Discuss the display and the different levels of the pond scene.

Help children brainstorm other things they might see at a pond. Start a chart with pictures and labels. Encourage children to add to it for the duration of the journey to the pond. Incorporate the words from the Pond Vocabulary list on page 132 whenever possible. Review the vocabulary words daily with the children.

Let's Go to the Pond! *(cont.)*

Procedure *(cont.)*

What could we do at the pond?

Review the five senses. Ask children about how they might use each sense when observing a pond. They might *see* floating water lilies, *hear* frogs croaking, *taste* freshwater fish that they have caught and cooked, *touch* furry cattails, and *smell* wildflowers.

Ask the children about possible pond activities they could participate in. *They could feed or count the ducks, skip rocks on the pond surface, fish, observe tadpoles, and collect smooth pebbles.*

When is the best time to visit the pond?

Ask children when they would visit a pond. *A good time to visit the pond might be spring when the weather starts to warm, flowers bloom, and baby mammals are born. Summer is also a nice time to take a trip to the pond because the days are longer, the plants grow taller, and the pond is bustling with all types of living creatures!*

What type of clothes would you wear?

Ask children what they should wear on the visit to the pond. *A pond is outdoors. You might choose to wear play clothes, such as blue jeans and sturdy shoes or boots. Wearing a rain jacket during the spring might be a good idea, just in case there is a rain shower!*

Why would you like to visit the pond?

Invite children to give reasons why they would like to visit a pond. *A pond is a special place where you can see plants, insects, amphibians, reptiles, mammals, birds, and fish who share the same environment as their home.*

Safety Note: Explain to children that they should practice safety rules around a real pond. They should not play around a pond without adult supervision. They should never go in the pond or drink the pond water.

Suggested Books

A Color of His Own by Leo Lionni

All Together Now by Anita Jeram

Beaver Pond Moose Pond by Jim Arnosky

Caterpillar and the Pollywog by Jack Kent

Come Along, Daisy! by Jane Simmons

Fine As We Are by Algy Craig Hall

From Egg to Butterfly by Marlene Reidell

Have You Seen My Duckling? by Nancy Tafuri

In the Small, Small Pond by Denise Fleming

Jump, Frog, Jump! by Robert Kalan

One Frog Sang by Shirley Parenteau

Splash by Ann Jonas

Waddle, Waddle, Quack, Quack, Quack by Barbara Anne Skalak

Pond Vocabulary

Mammals

beaver
deer
muskrat
otter
raccoon
shrew
skunk
vole

Fish

bass	perch
carp	pike
goldfish	stickleback
minnow	sunfish

Insects

ant	dragonfly
butterfly	grasshopper
cricket	mosquito
diving beetle	pond skater

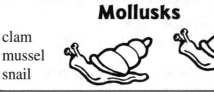

Birds

duck
egret
goose
heron
kingfisher
robin
swan

Mollusks

clam
mussel
snail

Reptiles

lizard   snake   turtle

Crustaceans

shrimp
water flea (daphnia)

Amphibians

frog	tadpole
newt	toad

Scavengers

crayfish
leech

Pond Plants

cattails	reeds
duckweed	rushes
grass	water lilies
iris	

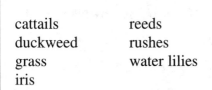

Other Pond Life

algae	flatworm
earthworm	spider

Pond Patterns

Above the Pond

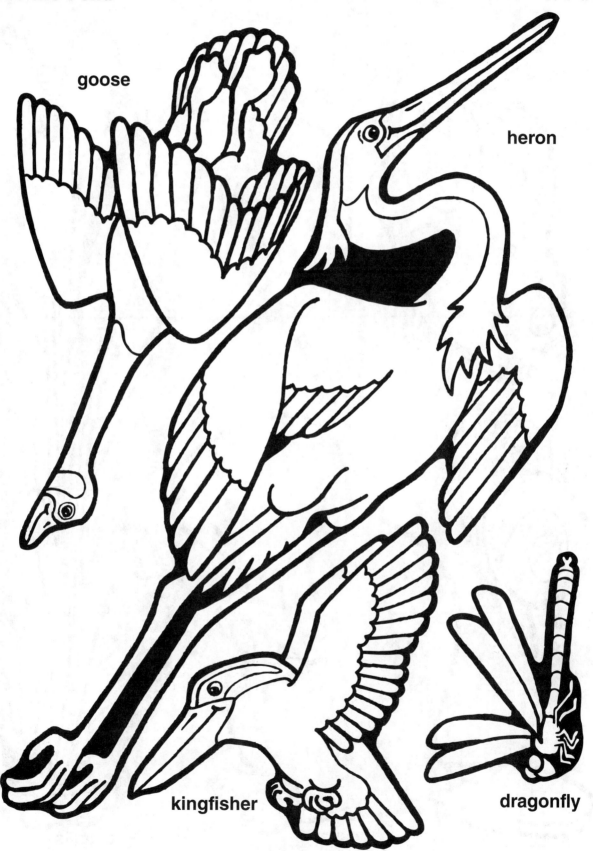

goose

heron

kingfisher

dragonfly

Pond Patterns *(cont.)*

Near the Pond

toad

shrew

snail

beaver

cattails

Pond Patterns *(cont.)*

Top of the Pond

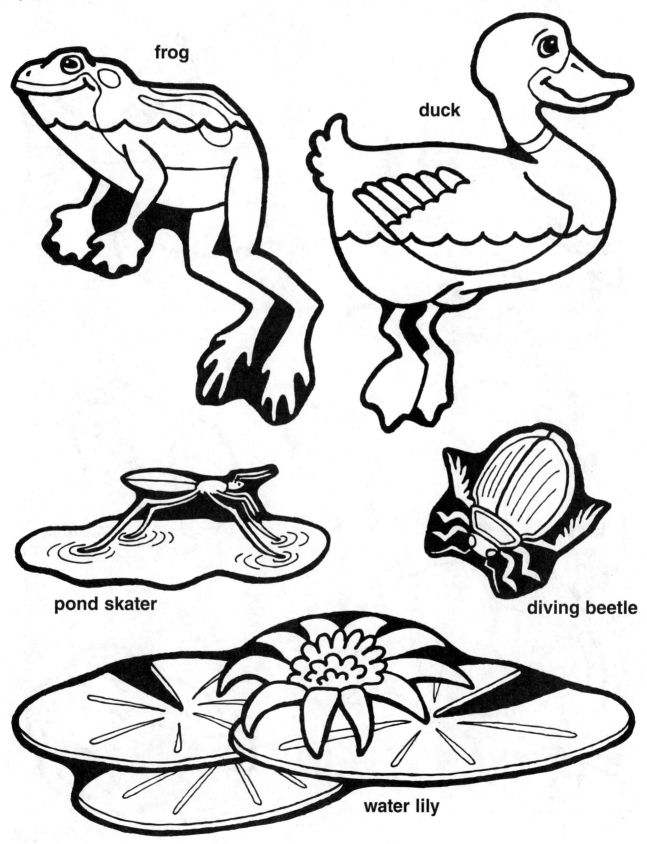

frog

duck

pond skater

diving beetle

water lily

Pond Patterns *(cont.)*

In the Pond

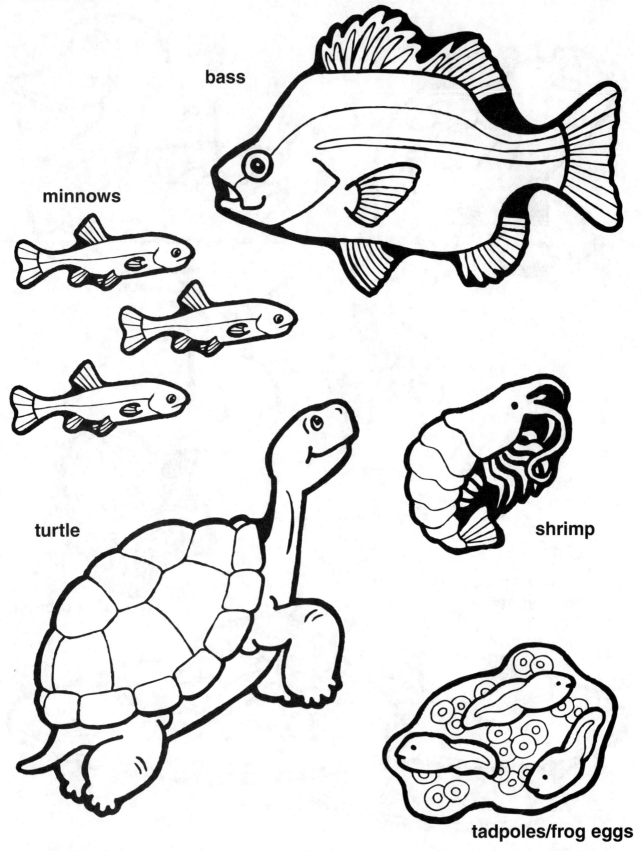

bass

minnows

turtle

shrimp

tadpoles/frog eggs

Pond Patterns *(cont.)*

Bottom of the Pond

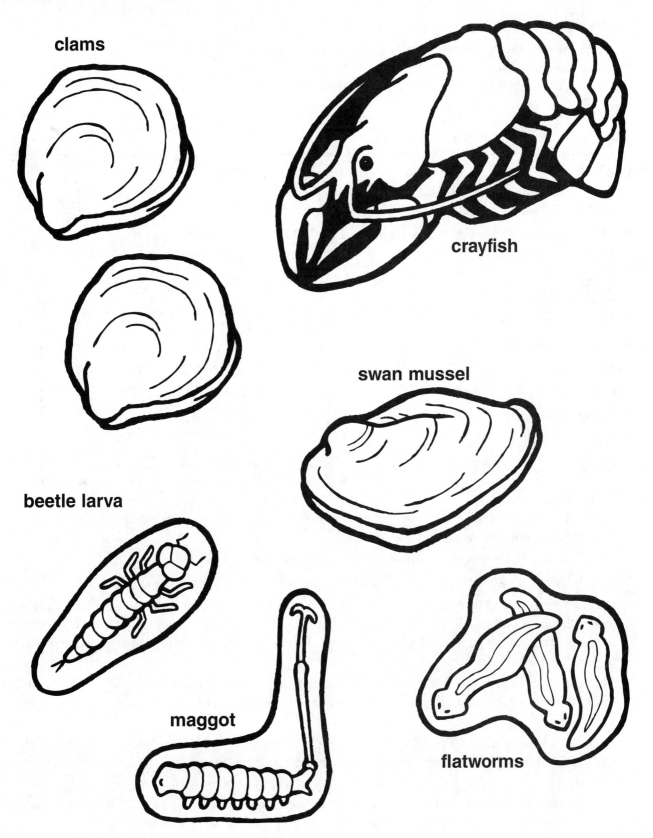

clams

crayfish

swan mussel

beetle larva

maggot

flatworms

"The Gingerbread Man"

— Readiness Standards —

Reading
- identifies the beginning sound of some words
- recognizes familiar print in the environment (e.g., stop sign)
- understands the difference between real (nonfiction) and make-believe (fiction/fantasy)

Science
- uses the senses to make observations

Materials

- "The Gingerbread Man" rhyming story poster on pages 140–141 or the color version, gingerbread man story.pdf, on the CD
- "The Gingerbread Man" Patterns on pages 142–143 or the color versions, gingerbread.pdf, on the CD
- "The Gingerbread Man" Story Scenes on pages 144–146 or the color versions, gingerbread scenes.pdf, on the CD
- X-acto® knife (teacher use only)
- hole punch
- craft sticks
- cardstock
- markers
- brads
- tape

Teacher Preparation

1. Copy "The Gingerbread Man" puppets and scenes onto cardstock or make color copies. Color, cut out, and laminate the puppets and scenes.

2. Using an X-acto knife, cut out the slit on each story scene.

3. Attach a craft stick to the back of a STOP sign to make a stick puppet.

4. Create a gingerbread man puppet by punching holes where indicated using a hole punch. Loosely attach the arms and legs to the gingerbread man puppet using brads. Carefully tape a craft stick to the back (to hold the puppet). Do not tape over the brads, as this will limit the leg and arm movements.

5. Create the fox puppet by punching holes where indicated using a hole punch. Attach the head and tail to the fox puppet using brads. Add a craft stick to this puppet using the same guidelines listed in step 4.

6. Read the rhyming story, "The Gingerbread Man." The more you read the story, the more children will be familiar with it and the more they will be able to participate.

   - **Preview** new vocabulary, such as *sigh*, *wails*, *shriek*, *yelps*, *twinkle*, *sly*, and *snatch*.
   - **Discuss/Practice** the refrains: "Stop, gingerbread man! I want to eat." "I'll run from you as fast as I can! ... catch me if you can. Bet you can't—I'm the gingerbread man!"

"The Gingerbread Man" (cont.)

Procedure

1. Explain to children that you will be reading a rhyming version, of "The Gingerbread Man" about a gingerbread man who meets several animals at a pond. Point out that each animal uses a different sense in the rhyme.

2. Hand out the gingerbread man puppet and beaver scene for the first stanza of the rhyming story. Explain to children that some of them will hold up the corresponding puppet or scene as the story unfolds.

3. Read the first stanza of "The Gingerbread Man" rhyming story to the group. Instruct the child holding the gingerbread man puppet to listen carefully to the words and slip the puppet into the corresponding scene after the beaver spots him and then, when appropriate, remove the puppet from the scene, wiggling the puppet's legs to show that he is running away from the beaver.

4. Collect the gingerbread man puppet and beaver scene and hand them different children for the next two stanzas of the story.

5. For the last two stanzas, give one child the gingerbread man and another child the fox.

6. Read the fourth and fifth stanzas of the rhyming story. Direct the children to use the gingerbread man and fox puppets and the bridge prop to act out the remainder of the story as you read it aloud to the class.

Revisiting the Rhyming Story

- Use the stop sign stick puppet. Reread the rhyming story to the group and have a different child hold up the stop sign each time the gingerbread man is told to stop by a character in the story.

- Discuss real *(nonfiction)* and make-believe *(fiction/fantasy)*. Ask the children, "What is real in this rhyming story?" *(Ducks swim in ponds—that is real.)* "What is make-believe?" *(Gingerbread cookies do not run—that is make-believe.)*

- Read the rhyming story aloud, pausing after one of the five senses is mentioned. Have the children point out which sense is mentioned in that section of the rhyming story: beaver *(sight)*, turtle *(smell)*, duck *(hearing)*, fox *(touch* and *taste)*.

- Discuss several words used to describe the animals in the rhyming story: *busy* (beaver), *big* (turtle), *little* (duck), and *sly* (fox). Encourage the children to guess why each describing word is an appropriate description for that animal. Challenge the children to tell which word in the story means the same as the word *tricky* (sly).

- Focus on some of the one-syllable words in the refrain. Either say the word slowly and ask children to name the beginning sounds (man-/m/) or emphasize the onset and rime of the words and see if children can blend them and name the words (n - o, *no*; m - an, *man*; r - un, *run*)

Character Concept

The gingerbread man's false sense of security and pride become his downfall!

Ask the children why it was a bad thing for the gingerbread man to be so sure of himself. *(He should have taken time to think about the situation before getting so close to the fox!)*

Talk to children about the importance of being humble and why one should not brag. Ask the children to think of ways they can show pride in themselves without bragging.

"The Gingerbread Man"

A busy beaver stops and sighs.
He sees a gingerbread man with his eyes.
"Stop, gingerbread man! I want to eat.
Come over here by my webbed hind feet."
"No!" wails the little gingerbread man.
"I'll run from you as fast as I can!
Busy beaver, catch me if you can.
Bet you can't—I'm the gingerbread man!"

A big green turtle rests by a pink rose,
She smells the gingerbread man with her nose.
"Stop, gingerbread man! I want to eat.
Come near the cattails and take a seat!"
"No!" shrieks the little gingerbread man.
"I'll run from you as fast as I can!
Big turtle, catch me if you can.
Bet you can't—I'm the gingerbread man!"

A big mallard duck quacks under a cloud,
He hears the gingerbread man talking aloud.
"Stop, gingerbread man! I want to eat.
Come in the water. Get out of the heat!"
"No!" yelps the little gingerbread man.
"I'll run from you as fast as I can!
Little duck, catch me if you can.
Bet you can't—I'm the gingerbread man!"

A sly fox sits on a bridge by some green moss.
She feels a gingerbread man's steps coming across.
The gingerbread man stops for the very first time.
He takes a quick breath and begins to rhyme.
"I've run from a beaver, a turtle, and a duck.
And I can outrun you with a little bit of luck."
The fox leans forward, telling the gingerbread man,
"Why don't you come closer? I'm not sure if you can!"

The gingerbread man approaches the sly fox.
He shouts while jumping like a jack-in-the-box.
"I've run from a beaver, a turtle, and a duck.
And I can run away from you as fast as a truck!"
"Really?" asks the fox with a twinkle in her eye.
The fox snaps up the gingerbread man before he can fly.
It looks like the gingerbread man has met his match.
Caught in the fox's mouth, he makes a tasty snatch!

"The Gingerbread Man" Patterns

Gingerbread Man and Props

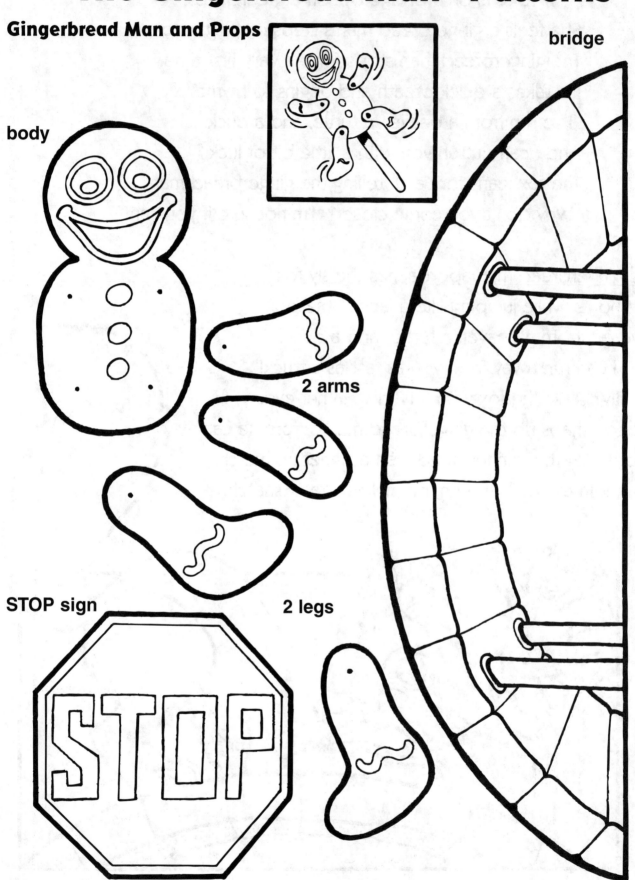

body

bridge

2 arms

STOP sign

2 legs

"The Gingerbread Man" Patterns *(cont.)*

Fox Puppet *(cont.)*

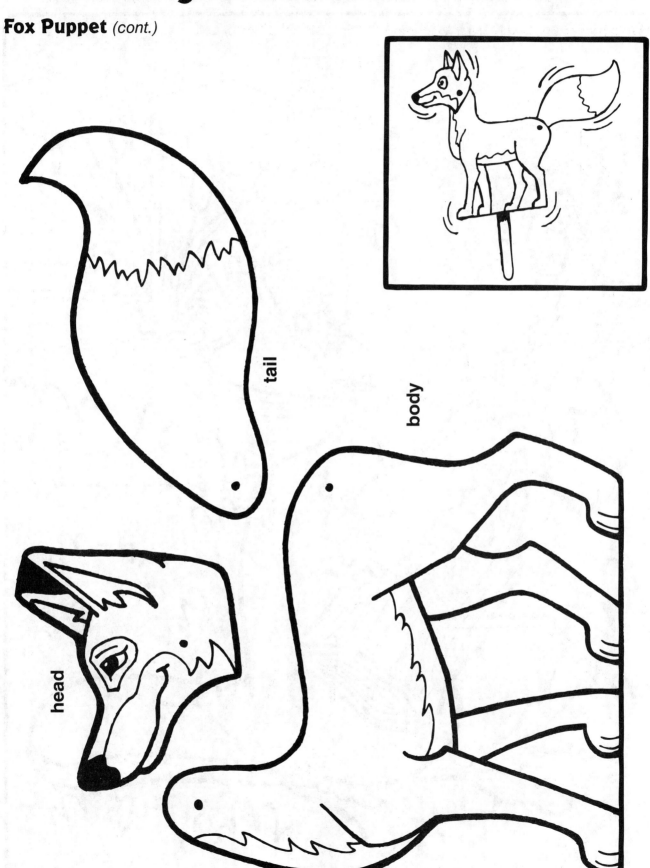

tail

body

head

"The Gingerbread Man" Scenes

"The Gingerbread Man" Scenes *(cont.)*

"The Gingerbread Man" Scenes *(cont.)*

Building Beaver Lodges

Readiness Standards

Fine Motor
- works with a variety of textures
- stacks blocks

Social
- solves problems while playing with others

Self-Help
- cleans up after a project

Materials
- wooden blocks
- pictures and books about beavers
- separate containers for building items
- pebbles, branches, sticks, pine needles
- beaver stuffed animal (optional)
- an enlarged version of the beaver lodge below or the color version, beaver lodge.pdf, on the CD

Teacher Preparation
1. Enlarge and photocopy the beaver lodge illustration or use the enlarged color version.
2. Gather books and pictures of beavers, dams, and lodges. If available, *Beaver Pond Moose Pond* by Jim Arnosky works well. If a stuffed beaver is not available, consider laminating a few pictures of beavers to use in the block area.
3. Place the materials at a block center and display the books and pictures nearby.

Procedure
1. Gather the children together and show them the illustration and pictures of beaver lodges. Read a story about beavers. Discuss with the children how beavers use logs, branches, sticks, and other materials around the pond to build their lodges. *Beavers use their sharp, orange front teeth to cut branches and gnaw on logs to create domed houses with underwater tunnels.*

2. Invite the children to visit the block center in small groups and use blocks and other materials to build a lodge for the stuffed beaver or beaver pictures.

3. Allow plenty of time for play when children finish constructing the lodge. Later, have them share it with you and explain what the beaver does in the lodge.

4. Encourage children to clean up the block center. Model how to sort the materials, placing the sticks in one container, the blocks in another container, etc. **Note:** This activity can be done outside in a dirt or sand area. Add water for a realistic touch!

Measuring Worms

Readiness Standards

Math	**Cognitive**	**Fine Motor**
• measures objects	• follows 2-step directions	• cuts out curved objects

Materials

- Worm Patterns on page 149 or the color versions, worm patterns.pdf, on the CD
- Measurement Strips below

Teacher Preparation

1. Copy and color the Worm Patterns or make color copies.
2. Copy and cut out a Measurement Strip for each child.

Procedure

1. Provide time for the children to cut out the worm patterns. While they are working, talk about the value of worms. Explain that worms are nature's recyclers, breaking down organic matter (*dead plants and animals*), which helps create richer soil. Also, as worms travel through the ground, they make tunnels that create paths for water to flow and roots to grow. (*aerators*)

2. Demonstrate to children how to measure a worm using the measurement strip.
   Hint: Measure the worm's length only.

3. Have children work in pairs, measuring one worm at a time. The first child measures a worm and tells his or her partner the size of the worm.

4. The second child checks the answer by repeating the measurement task.

5. The partners switch tasks and repeat steps 3–4 until all the worms have been measured.

Measurement Strips

1	2	3	4	5	6	7
1	2	3	4	5	6	7
1	2	3	4	5	6	7

Worm Patterns

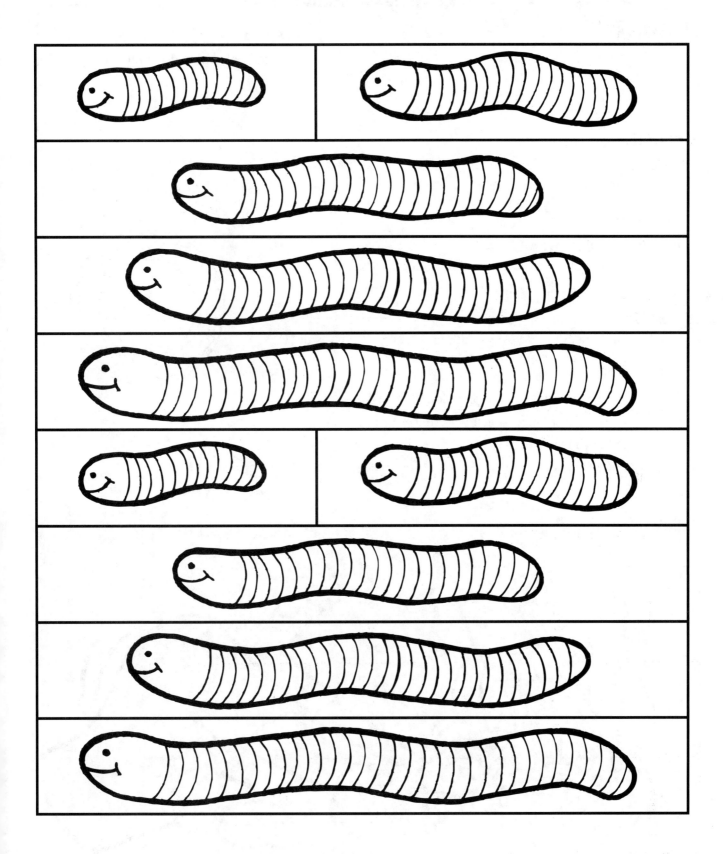

Caterpillar Shapes

Readiness Standards

Math

- recognizes shapes
- understands a shape's orientation in space can change

Fine Motor

- manipulates play dough to form shapes

Materials

- Caterpillar Shape Cards on page 151 or the color versions, caterpillar shapes.pdf, on the CD
- play dough or clay

Teacher Preparation

1. Copy and laminate the Caterpillar Shape Cards.
2. Place the materials at a center.

Procedure

1. Review shape names. Ask children if there are curves or flat sides on the shapes. Count the number of sides. Draw the shapes in the air.
2. Ask children to roll out the play dough to make caterpillars.
3. Bend the caterpillars on each pattern to form the shape.
4. Name the shape created.
5. Continue in this manner until each of the five shapes has been formed with dough.

Caterpillar Shape Cards

Mosaic Butterfly

Readiness Standards

Fine Motor
- tears paper into small pieces
- colors and pastes

Cognitive
- attends to adult-directed tasks for short periods of time

Materials
- Butterfly Pattern on page 153
- 4" black, brown, or beige chenille stick per child
- 2 or 3 half sheets of yellow, blue, orange, or purple construction paper for each child
- yarn (to hang projects)
- glue and glue brushes
- packing tape
- crayons

Teacher Preparation
1. Copy and cut out the Butterfly Pattern for each child. Cut the chenille sticks into 4" lengths.
2. Give each child a butterfly pattern, a chenille stick, and 2 or 3 half-sheets of construction paper.

Procedure
1. Ask the children what colors they received. Ask them to name other things that are the same colors.
2. Direct the children to tear the paper into small pieces. Explain that they will use these pieces to make a mosaic pattern on their butterflies.
3. Have each child spread glue on the butterfly shape and arrange the pieces on the butterfly pattern. Encourage children to make similiar (symmetrical) patterns on both sides.
4. When the glue is dry, let the child use crayons to add features to the butterfly.
5. Have children bend the chenille sticks in half and tape them to the back of the butterfly heads to create antennae.
6. Use packing tape to attach a length of yarn to the back of the butterfly to hang it from the ceiling.

Butterfly Pattern

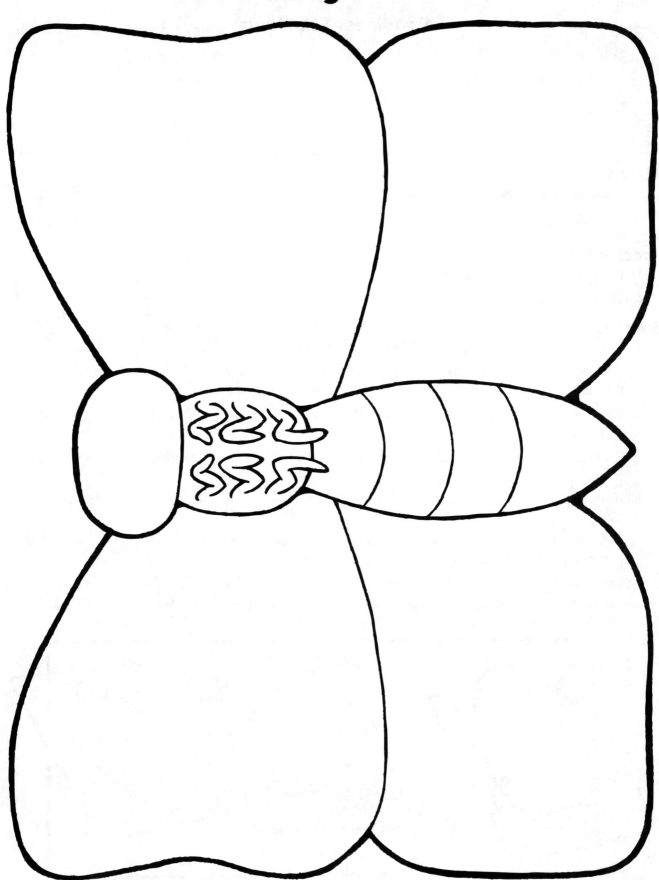

Pond Eggs

── Readiness Standards ──

Science
- knows that some baby animals come from eggs

Social
- cooperates with others

Oral Language
- speaks clearly

Materials
- Pond Animal Cards on page 155 or the color versions, pond animals.pdf, on the CD
- 6 plastic eggs

Teacher Preparation
1. Copy, color, and cut out the Pond Animal Cards or make color copies.
2. Place the cards and plastic eggs at a center.

Procedure
1. Review with children that birds and fish are types of animals that hatch from eggs.
2. Then ask the children if they know how baby insects, frogs, and turtles are born. Tell children that insects, frogs, and turtles are also animals that hatch from eggs.
3. Remind the children that mammals, such as raccoons, deer, and beavers, give birth to live babies.
4. Have children work in pairs. The first child selects an animal card.
5. If the card represents a pond animal baby that hatches from an egg, the child places a plastic egg on the card and says, " _____ come from eggs!"
6. If the card represents a pond baby that comes from a live birth, the child sets aside the card and says, " _____ don't come from eggs!"
7. The second child confirms if his or her partner's answer is correct, and repeats steps 4–6 with a remaining pond animal card.
8. Continue until all the plastic eggs have been placed on a pond animal that hatches from an egg.

   Note: You may wish to draw ovals on the backs of the cards featuring the animals that hatch from eggs. This would enable children to self-check.

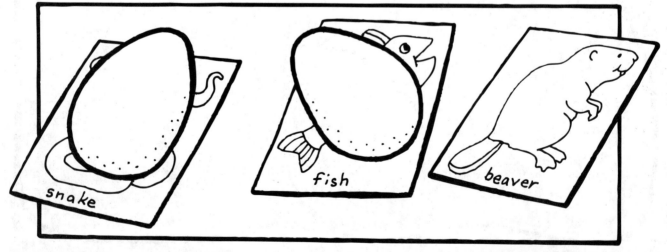

Pond Animal Cards

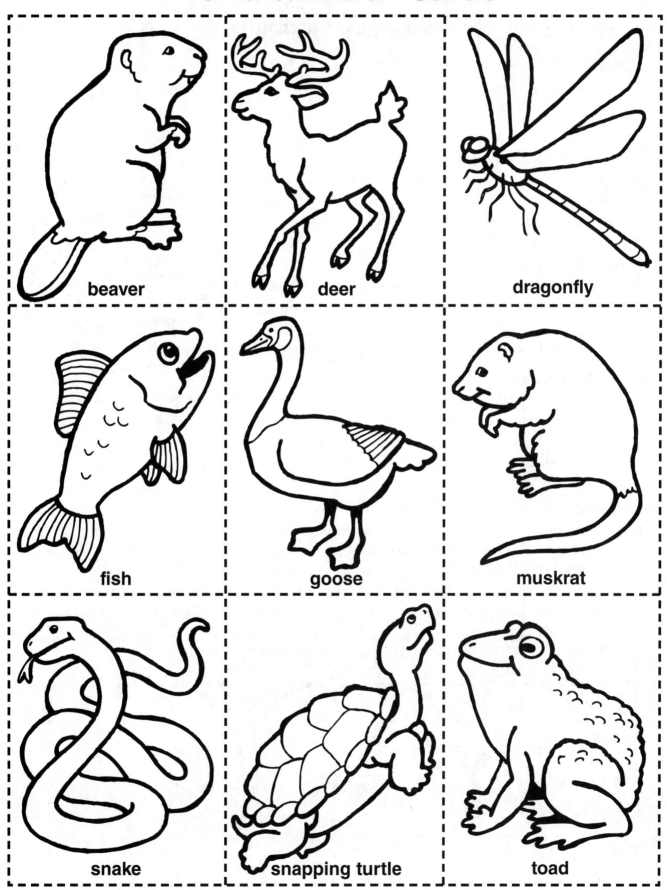

Ducks in a Row

Readiness Standards

Math

- sorts similar objects by color and size
- counts from 1 to 5

Fine Motor

- takes turns with a partner

Social

- uses pincer grasp to place and remove items

Materials

- water table (or large plastic tub) and access to water
- Number Cards (below)
- large white pom-poms
- small yellow pom-poms
- 2 containers
- 2–4 blunt-edged tweezers or tongs
- blue bulletin board paper (if water is not available)

Teacher Preparation

1. Place the white pom-poms in one container and the yellow pom-poms in the other container.
2. Fill the water table with an inch of water or cut the blue paper to suggest a pond.
3. Set the two pom-pom containers and tweezers near the pond. If appropriate, attach the number cards to the containers. Place the 1 on the white pom-pom container and the 5 on the yellow pom-pom container.

Procedure

1. Have children work in pairs. Each child selects one large white pom-pom (mama duck) and five small yellow pom-poms (baby ducks) from the container (nest) using their fingers or tweezers. Two groups may work at a time if the pond is large enough.
2. Each child will place one mama duck in the pond, and five baby ducklings trailing after her!
3. When finished, partners check each other to ensure that there are five ducklings and one mama.
4. The children remove the ducks, shake them off (like real ducks do!), and return them one at a time to the container (nest). **Note:** The wet ducks should still float.

Frog Frolic

Readiness Skills

Gross Motor
- leapfrogs, hops, and skips
- freezes in place after being in motion

Listening
- follows 1- and 2-step directions

Oral Language
- speaks clearly in front of class

Materials
- Lily Pad Spinner on page 158 or the color version, lily pad spinner.pdf, on the CD
- sheet of white cardstock
- paper clip
- pen

Teacher Preparation
1. Photocopy the Lily Pad Spinner onto cardstock, color, and cut it out or make a color copy.
2. Set the spinner on a table with the paper clip and the pen.

Procedure
1. Gather the children for large group time and tell them that they will take turns spinning the Lily Pad Spinner to determine which frog action the group will perform.

    Hop: Hop from one place to another in a leapfrog position.

    Sit: Freeze in place, pretending to sit on a log.

    Jump: Jump up and down in place. Jumping can be done standing or on all fours.

    Eat: Pretend to catch a fly by flicking one's tongue in and out.

2. The Teacher Frog invites a Child Frog to hop to the spinner and spin. The child uses the spinner by holding a pen upright on the X mark in the middle of the paper clip and giving a quick push (or flick) to the paper clip. Or, the teacher can hold the pen and the child can spin the clip.

3. After the child spins the spinner, he or she directs the class to perform that frog action.

4. The children perform the action as if they were frogs. Encourage them to make frog sounds.

5. Continue in the same manner, repeating steps 2–4, until each child has had the chance to spin the spinner and give a direction.

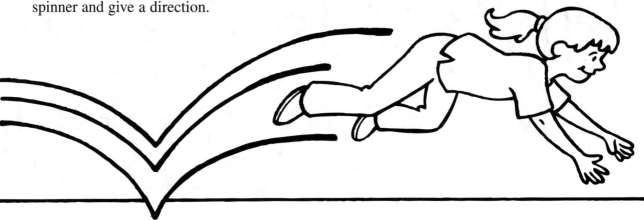

Lily Pad Spinner

Camouflaged Pond Critters
── Readiness Standards ──

Science
- understands that living things have similar needs (e.g., protection from predators)
- uses the senses to make observations about living things

Gross Motor
- hops and crawls

Materials
- Toad Pattern from page 134 or the color version, in the pond patterns.pdf, on the CD
- Lizard Pattern or the color versions, lizards.pdf, on the CD
- brown and green construction paper

Lizard Pattern

Teacher Preparation
1. Copy the Toad Pattern onto brown construction paper and the Lizard Pattern onto green construction paper and cut them out.
2. Place the toad on a brown item so it blends into its surroundings.
3. Place the lizard on a green item so that it blends into its surroundings.

Procedure
1. Explain the concept of camouflage. *Camouflage* is a coloring or behavior that helps an animal hide. Tell the children that many pond critters use camouflage to protect them from other animals that would like to eat them. Camouflaged animals have a better chance of staying alive! Explain that camouflage is not the same as hiding in or under something. Instead, camouflage is about blending into an area.
   Note: *A Color of His Own* by Leo Lionni explains this concept.
2. Discuss different brown pond objects that a brown toad could hide on (*log, tree trunk, soil*) to camouflage itself. Do the same for the lizard and name different green pond objects (*lily pad, grass, green leaves*). Tell children that a lizard and a toad are hiding in the classroom.
3. Allow each child to choose to look for the lizard or the toad. If looking for a toad, the child hops on the floor. If looking for a lizard, the child should crawl. Have each child sit down as soon as he or she finds one of the camouflaged animals. Then when all are seated, have them point to each animal in turn.
4. After children have spotted the lizard and the toad, talk about why it was hard to find them. Review with children why it would be beneficial for animals to blend into their surroundings.

Extension: Provide additional copies of the toads and lizards and encourage children to see if they can find areas outside where the animals will be camouflaged. At the end of the day, have children collect their animals if they have not already been found.

"One Little Goose"

Readiness Skills

Reading
- retells stories using props

Fine and Gross Motor
- performs finger movements
- dramatizes familiar rhymes

Materials
- Geese Puppets on page 161 or the color versions, geese.pdf, on the CD
- "One Little Goose" poem (below)
- markers
- tape
- craft sticks (optional)

Teacher Preparation
1. Copy, color, and cut out the Geese Puppets or make color copies to use in the demonstration.
2. Assemble the finger puppets by cutting and rolling the base of each puppet to fit and tape it into position.

Note: If making additional sets of puppets for each student, consider cutting only the outside border of each puppet and having children add craft sticks to the backs of their sets using tape. It might be too difficult for little hands to fit the five puppets on their fingers.

Procedure
1. Explain to children that they will be learning a variation of the traditional poem, "This Little Piggy." Say the rhyme a few times to get the rhythm going.
2. Read the new version, "One Little Goose," aloud several times.
3. Demonstrate to children how to use each finger puppet with its corresponding line.
4. Recite "One Little Goose" while featuring the finger puppet to act out the rhyme. After going through the poem a few times, the children can act out the lines of the poem—*swimming*, *drying off*, *eating plants*, *flying high*, and *honking*.
5. Later, have children take turns retelling the poem using the finger or stick puppets.
   Note: To aid them, the puppets have been numbered.

"One Little Goose"

One little goose swims quickly.
One little goose stays dry.
One little goose eats pond plants.
One little goose flies high.
One little goose cries, "Honk, honk, honk,"
All the day long.

Geese Puppets

"One Little Goose"

One little goose swims quickly.
One little goose stays dry.
One little goose eats pond plants.
One little goose flies high.
One little goose cries,
"Honk, honk, honk,"
All the day long.

Honk!
Honk!
Honk!

"Five Little Speckled Frogs"

Readiness Skills

Math
- knows common language for comparing quantity of objects (e.g., "less than," "same as")
- knows that quantity of objects can change by taking away objects

Gross Motor
- jumps from a crouching position

Materials
- "Five Little Speckled Frogs" poem (below)
- balance beam (or masking tape)

Teacher Preparation
1. Set up the balance beam in the classroom or make two long parallel lines on the floor, approximately six inches apart using masking tape.
2. Mark the left or right side in some way to indicate the side from which the frogs will jump in and hop away.

Procedure
1. Have children (in groups of five) take turns sitting on the log (balance beam).
2. As the rest of the class recites the poem, "Five Little Speckled Frogs," the five children on the log will act out the poem.
3. One "frog" jumps into the pool (from the designated side) during each verse.
4. Invite five different children to sit on the beam to be the frogs.
5. As the class recites the poem again, pause at the end of each verse. Ask how the total number of frogs has changed when one frog jumps off.
6. Discuss with the class if there are more frogs on the log now than there were at the beginning of the song. Are there fewer frogs? Is there the same number of frogs? Have the children explain why there are fewer frogs on the log each time.

"Five Little Speckled Frogs"

Five little speckled frogs sitting on a speckled log.
(Hold up 5 fingers while squatting down.)

Eating some most delicious bugs, yum, yum!
(Rub belly.)

One jumped into the pool,
where it was nice and cool,
(The child on the designated end jumps in and hops away.)

Then there were four speckled frogs, glump, glump.
(All say "glump, glump.")

Four little speckled frogs ...
(Continue until there are no frogs left.)

Souvenir Pond Pail

This is the culminating activity for the pond unit—the take-home souvenir! Assembling this project requires some prep time, depending on the students' cutting abilities and fine motor abilities. Adult assistance can be helpful, and will also provide children with more opportunities to share what they have learned about the pond as they work on the project. It is suggested that the pail be assembled on one day and the pond life on another.

Pond Pail

Materials

- School-Home Connection Ticket on page 167
- Pond Surface Patterns on page 167 or the color versions, pond surfaces.pdf, on the CD
- sheet of light blue cardstock for each child
- 9 oz. clear plastic cup for each child
- 12" chenille stick for each child
- hole punch

Teacher Preparation

1. Copy the School-Home Connection Ticket and the Pond Surface Pattern onto light blue cardstock for each child. Cut them out. Cut slits in the pond surface where marked.
2. Punch a hole into each School-Home Connection Ticket.
3. Punch two holes below the rim on each side of the clear plastic cups. This is where the pail handles will be inserted.

Procedure

1. Thread a chenille stick through one of the holes in the pail. Start from the outside of the cup.
2. Secure that end of the chenille stick inside the pail by twisting it. (Help students as needed.)
3. Slip the School-Home Connection Ticket through the other end of the chenille stick.
4. Thread the unsecured end of the chenille stick through the remaining hole in the pail and twist it closed to create the pail handle.

Pond Life

Materials

- Pond Life Patterns on pages 165–166 or the color versions, pond life patterns.pdf, on the CD
- sheet of white copy paper for each child
- sheet of white cardstock for each child

Teacher Preparation

1. Copy the Swimmers Patterns on page 165 onto white copy paper for each child or make color copies.

2. Copy the Critters Patterns on page 166 onto white cardstock for each child or make color copies.

Procedure

1. Color and cut out the Pond Life Swimmers patterns.
2. Color and cut out the Pond Life Critters patterns.

Souvenir Pond Pail *(cont.)*

Souvenir Pond Pail Assembly

Materials

- Pond Surface Pattern (page 167)
- Pond Pail
- Pond Life Patterns (pages 165–166)
- four 6 mm wiggly eyes for each child
- 4 small craft sticks for each child
- blue plastic wrap or 12" squares of cellophane
- glue sticks
- clear tape

Teacher Preparation

1. Provide each child with his or her completed pail, pond surface, and Pond Life Patterns.
2. Explain that they will be combining the items to finish the Souvenir Pond Pail.

Procedure – Stage 1 Under the Surface

1. Tape the Swimmers to the inside of the pail. The detailed side of the illustrations should face out.
2. Use a piece of blue plastic wrap to line the cup or crumple the cellophane and place it in the cup to suggest water.
3. Color the lily pad on the pond surface and tape it to the top of the pond (clear plastic cup).

Procedure – Stage 2 On the Surface

1. Glue a wiggly eye to each side of the frog. When the glue is dry, fold the frog on the dashed line, illustration side out, and tape it to a small craft stick.
2. Add a wiggly eye to each side of the duck. When the glue is dry, fold the duck on the dashed line, illustration side out, and tape it to a small craft stick.
3. Fold the cattail pattern, illustration side out, and tape it to a small craft stick.
4. Insert the frog puppet, duck, and cattail puppets into the holes on the pond surface.
5. Have children take home the Souvenir Pond Pails to share with family and friends.

School-Home Connection

Making the Pond Pail provides each child with a souvenir of the unit to take home to share what he or she has learned. By sending home this homemade souvenir, along with a copy of the School-Home Connection Ticket, each child will be encouraged to discuss what he or she has learned. Parents can use the prompts on the ticket as a springboard for discussions, songs, stories, and other activities from the pond unit.

Teacher Note: Don't forget to have an official passport stamping at the end of the pond journey.

Souvenir Pond Pail *(cont.)*

Pond Life Patterns

Swimmers Patterns

crayfish

turtle

fish

minnow

Swimmers Patterns

crayfish

turtle

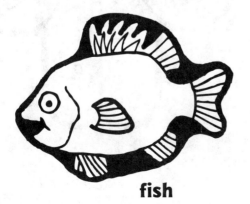

fish

minnow

Souvenir Pond Pail *(cont.)*

Pond Life Patterns *(cont.)*

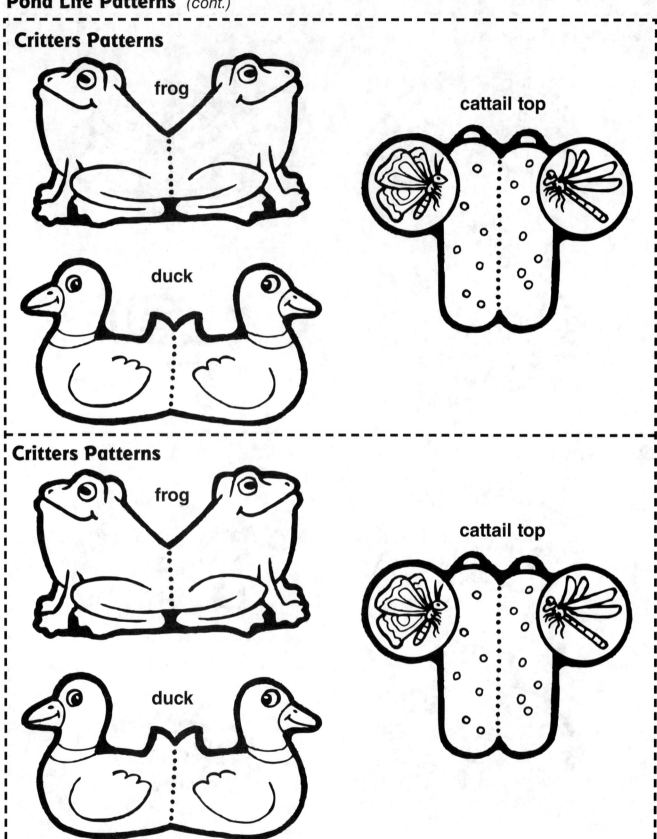

Critters Patterns

frog

cattail top

duck

Critters Patterns

frog

cattail top

duck

Souvenir Pond Pail *(cont.)*

Pond Surface Patterns

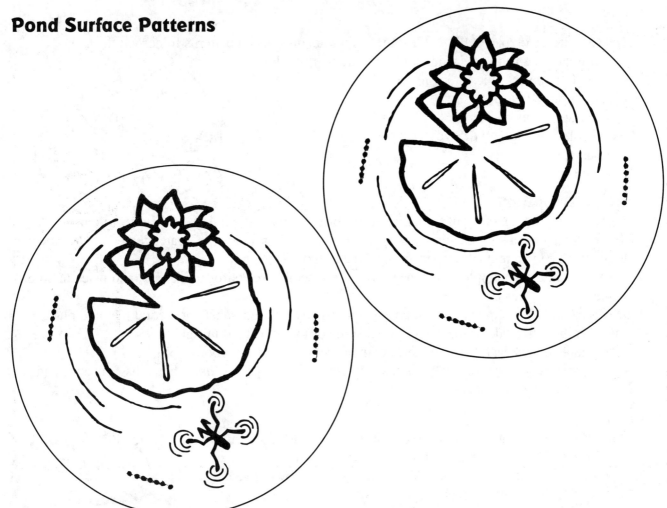

School-Home Connection Ticket: Pond

Our class has just finished a study of the pond. Each day we learned more about pond life. Take a look at your child's Pond Pail souvenir from our "visit" to the pond. Find out what he or she learned. You might start by discussing the following:

Which pond animal or insect ...

       —is your favorite?

       —has a baby called a tadpole (*duckling/hatchling/fry (fish)/pup (seal)*)?

       —makes the sound *quack* (*ribbit/buzz/hiss/honk*)?

       —swims (*skates/crawls/leaps/flutters*)?

       —has feathers (*scales/skin/wings/legs*)?

Which pond plant ...

       —makes a good place for animals to rest?

       —is tall with a brown, furry top?

       —has a white flower on it?

Let's Go to the Ocean!

Materials

- Ocean Patterns on pages 171–177 or the color versions, ocean patterns folder, on the CD
- ocean-related items (e.g., sand, shovel, plastic fish, shells)
- blue bulletin board paper or poster board
- brightly colored paper
- brown paper bags, all sizes
- wooden blocks (variety of sizes)
- sand bucket
- tape and scissors

Teacher Preparation

1. Copy and color a class set of Ocean Patterns, or use the color version, and cut them out.
2. To create an ocean scene, cut a length of blue bulletin board paper. Create an area on the floor or a display area where it can be set up for the duration of the unit.
3. Have the children crumple brown paper bags to resemble rocks for a tide pool and place them on one end of the ocean.
4. Have the children help cut coral shapes from brightly colored paper for a coral reef and place them on the other side of the ocean. Fold some of them to stand upright.
5. Using tape, attach each ocean pattern to an appropriately sized wooden block.
6. Collect a variety of ocean-related items (e.g., sand shovel, plastic fish, shells, bag of sand) and place them in a sand bucket.

Procedure

1. Have the children sit in a close group. It is important for all children to see the visual aids and hear the responses from classmates.
2. Introduce the unit on ocean life by presenting the following visuals, simple questions, and facts about the ocean.

Where are we going?

Explain to the children that they will be learning about oceans and beaches.

They will be reading about ocean life, and learning even more about ocean plants and animals. They will learn many new things that will help them imagine that they are part of a real ocean and beach!

Read an ocean-themed book to the children. Use a classroom favorite or choose a new one from the Suggested Books listed on page 169. Show the children a collection of ocean-related items in a sand bucket. Ask them where they think these things are found. Then explain to the children that they will be studying oceans. Ask them what they know about oceans. *An ocean is a body of salt water. Oceans cover most of the earth!* Invite children who have visited an ocean to briefly describe their experiences.

Who/what will we see at the ocean?

Display the ocean scene on a table so that it is visible to all. Discuss the display and the different parts of the ocean scene (*tide pool, open ocean, coral reef*). Ask the children who or what they might see at the ocean. *They might see beachcombers, surfers, fish, shells, crabs, sand, seaweed, and large waves!* Help the children brainstorm other things they might see at an ocean. Start a chart with pictures and labels. Encourage the children to add to it for the duration of the journey to the ocean. Incorporate the words from the Ocean Vocabulary list on page 170 whenever possible. Review the vocabulary words daily with the children.

Let's Go to the Ocean! *(cont.)*

Procedure *(cont.)*

Who/what will we see at the ocean? *(cont.)*

Share with the children the following information about the parts of the ocean. After discussing a part, place the corresponding ocean blocks on the appropriate area of the scene. Talk about animals that must stay in water to live *(e.g., fish, shark, moray eel)*, animals that live in water but breathe air *(e.g., dolphin, whale)*, and animals that live in and out of water *(e.g., sea turtle, fiddler crab, sea star)*.

Tide pools form near rocks at the edge of the ocean. Ocean waves wash into and out of the pools, bringing fresh water and food. Tide pool animals stay attached to their rocks and do not get washed out to sea by attaching permanently or moving about using sticky "feet" *(e.g., sea star, sea urchin)*.

Coral reefs are homes for many ocean plants and animals. Coral reefs are usually located in warm, shallow water because tiny plants that support coral growth need sunlight.

Open ocean currents are always moving and are home to some of the smallest and largest animals on Earth. Animals in the open ocean have no place to hide. Those that may be eaten protect themselves by swimming together in large groups. Many open ocean animals feed on krill and plankton.

What could we do at the ocean?

Review the five senses. Ask the children about how they might use each sense when observing an ocean and beach. They might *see* crabs scurrying in the sand, *hear* the calls of seabirds, *taste* the salty ocean water, *touch* warm sand or smooth shells, and *smell* dried seaweed. Ask the children about possible ocean activities they could participate in. *They could wade in the ocean, swim, fish, go sailing, observe ocean animals, surf, and collect shells.*

When is the best time to visit the ocean?

Ask the children when they would visit an ocean. *Summer is a nice time to visit the ocean. The days are long and warm, and the beach is a perfect vacation spot!*

What type of clothes would you wear?

Ask children what they should wear on the visit to the ocean. *An ocean is outdoors. You might choose to wear shorts, a short-sleeved shirt, or sandals. If you plan to get wet, wear a swimsuit! Wear sunglasses to protect your eyes, and a sun hat and sunscreen to protect your skin from the sun's rays.*

Why would you like to visit the ocean?

Invite children to give reasons why they would like to visit an ocean. *An ocean is a special place where you can see animals that live in and around the water. You might even find a beautiful sea star or shell.*

Safety Note: Explain to the children that they should practice safety rules around a real ocean. They should not play in or around an ocean without adult supervision.

Suggested Books

A House for Hermit Crab by Eric Carle
At the Beach by Anne Rockwell
Beach Party! by Harriet Ziefert
Fish Eyes by Lois Ehlert
One Sun: A Book of Terse Verse
   by Bruce McMillan
One White Wishing Stone: A Beach Day Counting Book by Doris Gayzagian

Sea, Sand, Me! by Patricia Hubbell
The Seashore Book by Charlotte Zolotow
Secret Sea Horse by Stella Blackstone
There Was an Old Lady Who Swallowed a Shell!
   by Lucille Colandro

Ocean Vocabulary

Seasonal

hot
humid
sandals
summer
sun hat
sunglasses
swimsuit

Ocean Activities

boating	snorkeling
chasing waves	surfing
fishing	swimming

Beach Activities

building sandcastles
collecting shells
playing beach ball
sunbathing

Sand Textures

coarse	grainy	rough	squishy
fine	packed	soft	

Open Ocean

Mammals	**Fish**	**Birds**	**Other Animals**
blue whale	great white shark	albatross	jellyfish
dolphin	swordfish	petrel	manta ray
sea lion	tuna	**Ocean Plants**	plankton
Reptile	**Mollusk**	kelp	
sea turtle	squid	seaweed	

Coral Reef

Fish	**Mollusks**	**Crustaceans**	**Other Animals**
clownfish	clam	lobster	anemone
puffer fish	oyster	shrimp	coral
sea horse	sea slug	**Birds**	moray eel
stingray		roseate tern	sponge

Tide Pool

Echinoderms	**Crustacean**	**Mollusks**	**Plants**
sand dollar	fiddler crab	mussel	sea lettuce
sea star	**Birds**	octopus	**Other Animal**
sea urchin	seagull	turban snail	sea anemone
	pelican		

Ocean Patterns

Tide Pool Patterns

sea anemone

sea lettuce

sea star

octopus

Ocean Patterns *(cont.)*

Tide Pool Patterns *(cont.)*

gull

turban snail

fiddler crab

mussel

Ocean Patterns *(cont.)*

Coral Reef Patterns

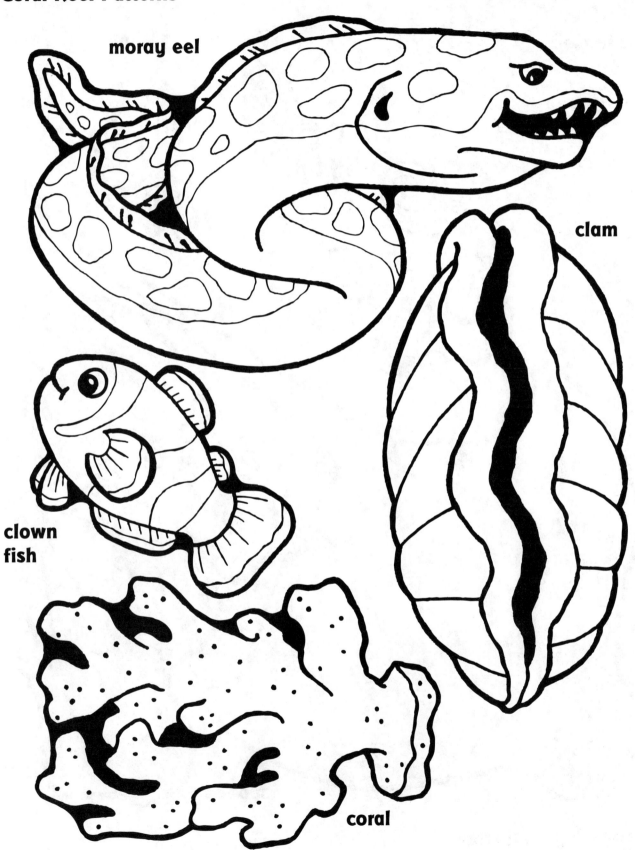

moray eel

clam

clown
fish

coral

Ocean Patterns (cont.)

Coral Reef Patterns (cont.)

sea horses   shrimp

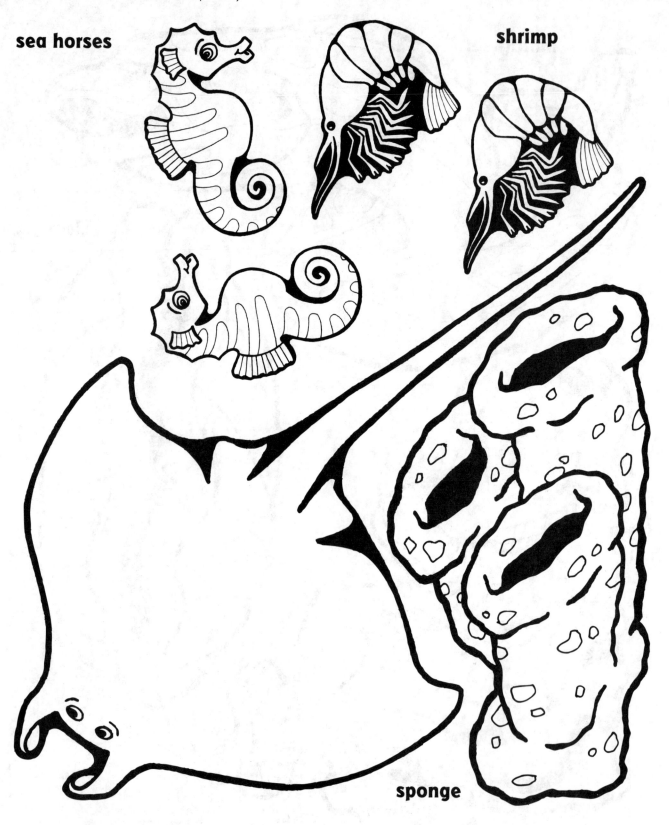

sponge

stingray

Ocean Patterns *(cont.)*

Open Ocean Patterns

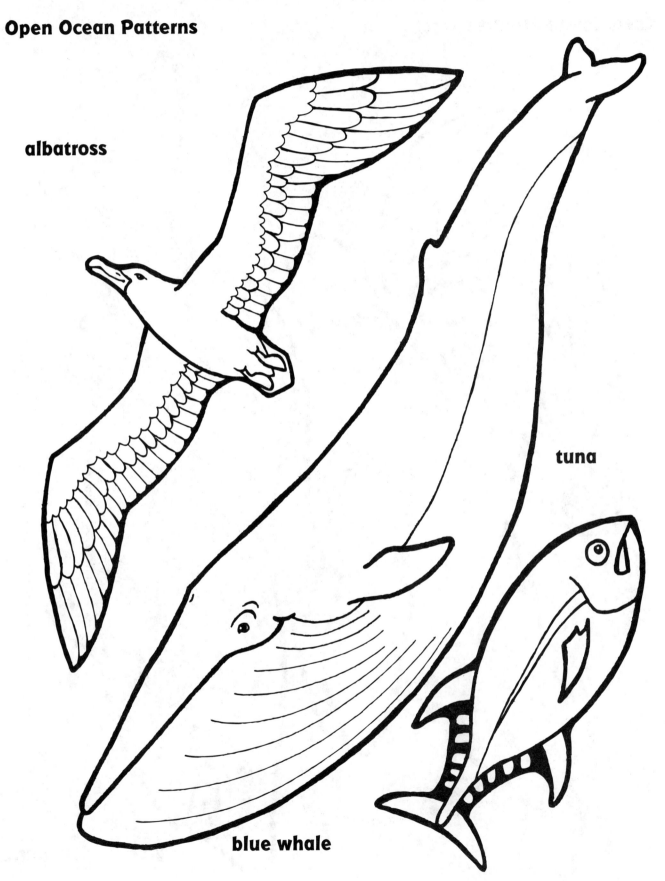

albatross

tuna

blue whale

Ocean Patterns *(cont.)*

Open Ocean Patterns *(cont.)*

jellyfish

sea lion

great white shark

Ocean Patterns *(cont.)*

Open Ocean Patterns *(cont.)*

dolphin

sea turtle

krill

plankton

"The Three Hermit Crabs Tough"

Readiness Standards

Reading

- uses emergent reading skills to "read" a story (e.g., gathers meaning from words and pictures)
- replaces initial sounds of words to create new words (i.e., *zubble* for *bubble*)
- understands the literal meaning of a story

Oral Language

- speaks expressively (e.g., uses different voices for various characters)

Materials

- "The Three Hermit Crabs Tough" rhyming story poster on pages 180–181 or the color version, hermit crab story.pdf, on the CD
- Shark Puppets on pages 183–184 or the color versions, sharks.pdf, on the CD
- 3 Hermit Crabs Tough Puppets on page 182 or the color versions, hermit crabs.pdf, on the CD
- X-acto® knife (teacher use only)
- large craft stick
- cardstock
- markers
- tape

Teacher Preparation

1. Copy the three hermit crab puppets onto cardstock or make color copies. Color the puppets and cut them out.

2. Have an adult use an X-acto knife to cut out the finger holes on each crab puppet prior to use.

3. To create the double-sided shark puppet, attach the sleeping shark pattern to a large craft stick and the awakened shark pattern to the reverse side of the craft stick.

4. Plan to spend a few days immersing students in the new ocean-themed, rhyming variation of "The Three Billy Goats Gruff" story.

5. Read the rhyming story, "The Three Hermit Crabs Tough." The more you read the story to the children, the more they will be familiar with it and the more they will be able to participate.

   - **Preview** new vocabulary, such as *grumbles*, *commotion*, *chow*, *clatter*, and *scurries*, with the children.
   - **Discuss** the refrains: "Don't bother with me; It's my bigger brother you have to see!" and "Who is walking across my beach now?"

"The Three Hermit Crabs Tough" *(cont.)*

Procedure

1. Explain to the children that you will be reading a rhyming version, of "The Three Billy Goats Gruff," which is about a mean, hungry shark and three hermit crabs that want to cross the beach.

2. Give the Little Hermit Crab puppet to a child. Have the child place the puppet on his or her other hand by inserting two fingers (index and middle fingers) through the holes. Demonstrate how to make the crabs walk if necessary.

3. Give the shark puppet to another child. Have him or her start by holding up the side that shows the shark sleeping.

4. Read the first and second stanzas of "The Three Hermit Crabs Tough" rhyming story to the group. Have the child with the shark puppet rotate it to show the shark wake up and the child with the crab puppet use his or her fingers to quickly crawl past the shark after he or she is allowed to.

5. Pause after reading the second stanza. Ask the children if Little Crab really means for the shark to eat his older brothers, or if they think Little Crab is just trying to trick the shark.

6. Give the shark and medium crab puppets to different children. Repeat steps 2–4 using the third and fourth stanzas of "The Three Hermit Crabs Tough" Rhyming Story.

7. Give the shark and big crab puppets to different children. Repeat steps 2–4 using the fifth and sixth stanzas of "The Three Hermit Crabs Tough" Rhyming Story.

8. Hand out the shark and big crab puppets to different children. Read the last two stanzas of the rhyming story to the group. Have the child with the crab puppet bump the shark puppet so that he falls back into the ocean.

9. Allow three other children to use the three crab finger puppets to show the crab brothers reuniting on the beach.

Revisiting the Rhyming Story

Once children are familiar with the rhyming story, "The Three Hermit Crabs Tough," try the following activities:

1. Have several children retell the story using the crab and shark puppets. Encourage the children to use a different voice for each character—Little Crab might speak with a baby voice; Big Crab might speak with a gruff voice.

2. Focus on the refrain, "Don't bother with me; It's my bigger brother you have to see!" Demonstrate to the children how to replace the initial sound of the word *me* to create new words (*be, gee, he, key, pea, see, tea, we*). Then ask the children to give replacements for the initial sounds of other words in the refrain: *my, you, to*, and *see*.

3. Share with the children the following words that describe Shark: *grumbles, upset, angrily*. Ask the children, "What do these words tell us about the shark in the rhyming story?" Discuss how important it is to pay attention to words that describe characters and how that helps the reader understand the story.

Character Concept

The three hermit crab brothers showed that a goal is reachable with patience and persistence; they made a hard job look easy! Direct the children to think about a time when they accomplished something that at first seemed very difficult to do. Invite several children to share how it made them feel when they completed the difficult task.

"The Three Hermit Crabs Tough"

Little Hermit Crab crosses the beach—*trip trap*.
He makes enough noise to wake Shark from his nap!
Shark asks, "Who is walking across my beach now?
That is something I will not allow!"

Says Little Hermit Crab, "Don't bother with me;
It's my bigger brother you have to see!"
Shark grumbles and lets Little Crab cross.
Shark goes back to sleep on a pillow of moss.

Medium Hermit Crab comes next—*trip trap*.
The commotion awakes Shark in a snap.
Shark asks, "Who is walking across my beach now?
I am getting hungry; I would like some chow!"

Says Medium Hermit Crab, "Don't bother with me;
It's my bigger brother you have to see!"
Shark swims away and lets Medium Crab cross.
Shark falls asleep, upset with his loss.

Big Hermit Crab is the last to come— **trip trap**.
His noisy claws make a clatter and a clap!
Shark says, "Who is walking across my beach now?
I think I know who it might be, somehow!"

Says Big Hermit Crab, "Don't bother with me!
I'm the Hermit Crab Tough, greatest of all three."
Shark growls angrily, "I'm going to eat you!
I've already missed out on quite a few."

Shark starts to chase Big Hermit Crab with the call,
"Come back Big Crab, I'll eat you shell and all!"
With his pair of claws, Big Crab pinches Shark,
Then Shark falls back into the deep ocean dark.

Big Hermit Crab misses his little brothers,
So he scurries along the sand to join the others.
The three Hermit Crabs Tough have crossed the beach,
And they now live safely out of hungry Shark's reach!

"The Three Hermit Crabs Tough" (cont.)

Little Crab puppet

Medium Crab puppet

Big Crab puppet

"The Three Hermit Crabs Tough" *(cont.)*

Shark Puppet

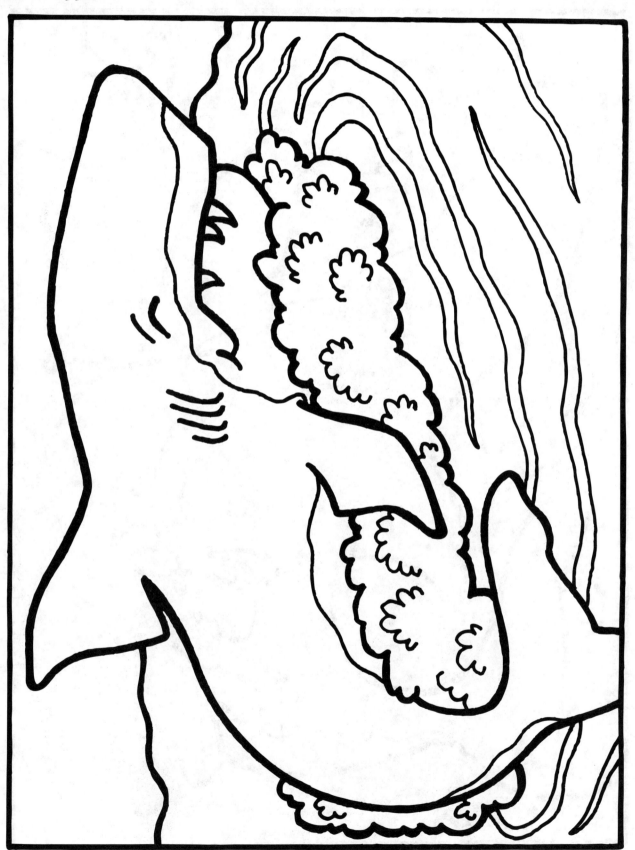

"The Three Hermit Crabs Tough" *(cont.)*

Shark Puppet *(cont.)*

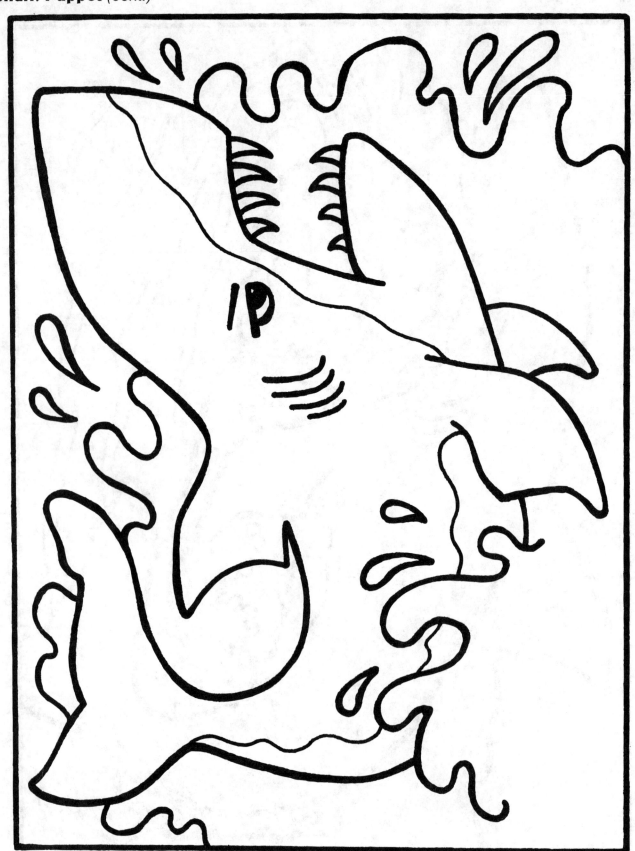

Sorting Seashells
Readiness Standards

Math
- sorts similar objects by attribute (e.g., smooth, rough, white, spotted)

Fine Motor
- works with a variety of textures

Materials
- variety of smooth and rough shells (available at craft stores)
- sand table or large, flat container filled with sand
- 2 small containers or sand buckets
- 2 sand shovels
- small piece of wax paper
- small piece of sandpaper

Teacher Preparation
1. Obtain or purchase a variety of sizes and textures of shells.
2. Tape the sandpaper on one container and the wax paper on the other container.
3. Gather the shells, containers, and sand shovels, and place them at the sand table center.

Procedure
1. At group time, allow the children to examine the shells and discuss them. Explain that shells are protective coverings for some animals.
2. Place the shells in the sand table and allow children to come to the center in pairs.
3. Each child digs in the sand with a sand shovel to look for shells.
4. When a child finds a shell, he or she will feel it to determine if the shell is rough or smooth.
5. If the shell is rough, the child will place it in the sandpaper container. If the shell is smooth, it is placed in the wax paper container. Continue in this manner until all the shells have been found and sorted into the appropriate container.

Shell Names
Readiness Standards

Writing
- uses writing tools and materials (e.g., pencils, markers)
- explores tracing words

Fine Motor
- uses pincer grasp to pick up small objects

Materials
- shell-shaped pasta
- glue
- tagboard or heavy paper

Teacher Preparation
Write each child's name on a separate piece of tagboard.

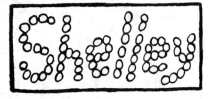

Procedure
1. Have each child trace over his or her name using a pencil.
2. Instruct the child to trace over one letter with glue.
   Then have the child attach shell-shaped pasta to the glue to form the letter.
3. Direct the child to repeat step 2 for each letter in his or her name and set the project aside to dry.

Patterning Beach Towels

Readiness Standards

Math
- completes patterns with objects (ABAB)
- recognizes groups of 1, 2, 3, and 4 objects

Social
- follows rules of a game

Fine Motor
- uses clothespins to attach objects to a line

Materials

- Towel Patterns on page 187 or the color versions, towel patterns.pdf, on the CD
- 2 sheets of white cardstock
- spring-type clothespins
- two chairs
- length of yarn

Teacher Preparation

1. Copy two sets of Towel Patterns onto white cardstock or make color copies. Color the towel patterns and cut them out.
2. Create a clothesline at a center using two chairs and a piece of yarn. Tie each end of the yarn to a different chair; then pull the chairs apart so the yarn is taut.
3. Gather the towel patterns and clothespins and place them at the center.

Procedure

1. To play the game, pairs work together to hang up beach towels on a clothesline at a center. The first child uses the clothespins to hang up two different patterned beach towels on the clothesline (AB pattern).
2. The second child selects and pins up the correct beach towels to finish the ABAB pattern.
3. The work is checked, the beach towels are removed from the clothesline, and the second child repeats Step 1.

Variation: Children may find matching beach towels and hang them together on the clothesline.

Extension: Encourage children to come up with ABCABC patterns on the line.

Towel Patterns

Ocean Scene
Readiness Standards

Fine Motor
- finger paints
- works with a variety of art media
- cuts and pastes

Cognitive
- works independently

Materials
- Orca Pattern on page 189
- blue, green, and turquoise powder paints
- smocks or old shirts (one per child)
- water
- flour
- glue
- heavy paper or finger paint paper
- markers or crayons
- large bowl
- 3 smaller bowls
- spoons
- colored scrap paper and markers (optional)

Teacher Preparation
1. Copy the Orca Pattern for each child.
2. In a large bowl, make a paste by mixing one part water and one part flour together, stirring constantly.
3. Divide the paste into several smaller bowls and add a different color of powder paint to each bowl to make finger paint.
4. Dampen the table top of a work area so the papers will not slip.
5. Place a heavy sheet of paper on the work area. Put some finger paint on each sheet of paper. Colors can be mixed if desired.

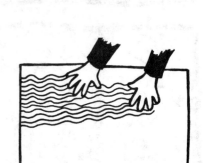

Procedure
1. Invite each child to slide his or her fingers through the finger paint to cover the paper (ocean). Encourage them to move their fingers smoothly like waves, creating ripples. Other children may prefer more "turbulent" movements. Ask them to describe the motions using terms associated with the ocean.
2. Set the ocean background papers aside to dry.
3. Have each child color, cut out, and glue an orca onto the dried painted background to create an ocean scene.
4. Allow children to complete their scenes by adding details using pieces of colored scrap paper, small shells, sand, and markers, if desired.

Orca Pattern

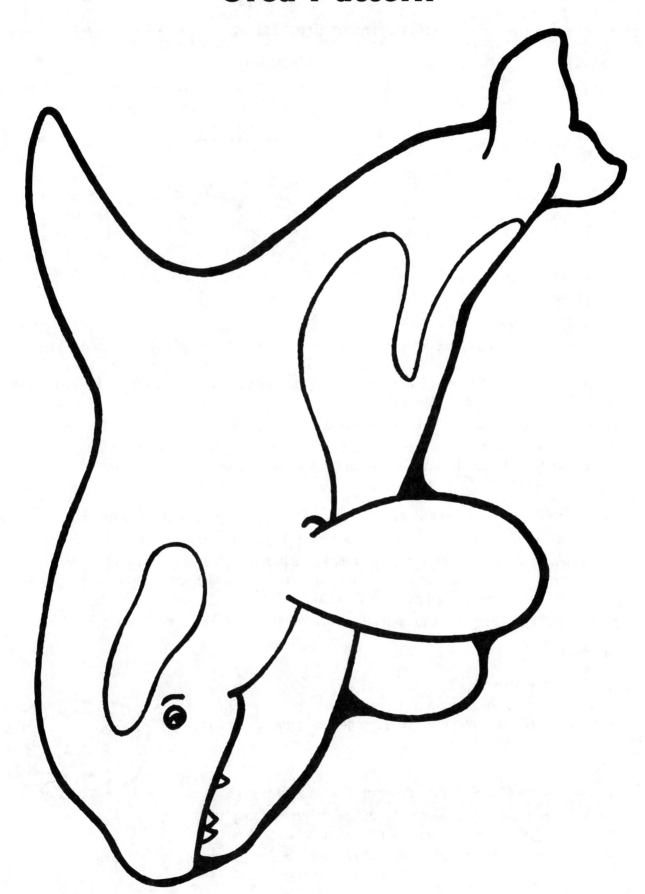

Beach Day

Readiness Standards

Social

- participates in cooperative play
- dramatizes situations with peers

Listening

- understands basic conversational vocabulary
- listens for a variety of purposes (to converse with a peer)

Materials

- water table or a small wading pool
- sand area or table
- beach toys (e.g., sand buckets and shovels)
- plastic ocean creatures and mammals
- rope
- beach umbrella (optional)

- shorts
- sun hats
- sunglasses
- beach towels
- seashells
- flip-flops

Beach Area

Teacher Preparation

1. Rope off a section of the outdoor play area to create a Beach Area. Add beach toys and other appropriate beach items. If a sand area is not available, create a sand table. **Note:** Clean play sand can be purchased at large hardware stores in the garden section. Add the sand to a large, low plastic container or a small, plastic pool.

2. Bury shells in the sand area for children to find.

3. Arrange a "beach" where beach towels can be spread out on a grassy or sandy area. If appropriate, add a beach umbrella. Arrange a second area for the water table/ocean.

Procedure

1. Review with the children what types of clothes would be appropriate to wear to the beach.

2. Talk with the children about what types of activities they might participate in at the beach.

3. At the Beach Area, allow time for small groups of children to pretend they are at the beach. Allow time for trying on the summer clothes provided, lying on the beach towels, playing in the sand, building sandcastles, collecting shells, etc.

4. Encourage the children to talk to each other about what they are doing while at the Beach Area.

Ocean Area

Teacher Preparation

Set aside an area for ocean creatures (*e. g., plastic fish, turtles, sea stars, and crustaceans*) and ocean mammals (*e. g., whales, dolphins*). A water table will work.

Procedure

1. Review with the children types of animals they might see at an ocean.

2. At the Ocean Area, allow time for the children to pretend they are at the ocean, sightseeing ocean creatures and mammals.

3. Encourage the children to talk to each other about what they are seeing at the Ocean Area.

Sandy Sea Star

Readiness Skills

Science
- uses the senses to make observations

Fine Motor
- works with a variety of textures
- cuts and pastes
- traces and colors

Materials
- Sea Star Pattern on page 192
- sheets of sandpaper (variety of grits)
- real sea star
- heavy cardstock
- shells
- crayons
- colored sand and glue (optional)

Teacher Preparation
1. Copy the Sea Star Pattern onto the cardboard. Make an appropriate number of patterns.
2. Arrange the project materials at a center.

Procedure
1. Allow the children to feel a real sea star, if available. Explain that real sea stars are fragile and should be handled with care.
2. Talk with the children about sea stars and how they feel. Discuss why the sea stars might have a rough texture. (*Spines are a protection from predators; they also aid in movement.*)
3. Have the children compare and contrast the texture of the sea star with some of the shells.
4. At a center, have the children run their fingers over a variety of sheets of sandpaper to feel the different textures (grits). Ask them which type of sandpaper they think feels most like a sea star.
5. Each child should select a sheet of sandpaper to complete his or her sea star project.
6. Each child places the desired sheet of sandpaper under a sea star pattern and traces the pattern. Children can work in pairs to help each other hold and trace the pattern.
7. Then, he or she uses a crayon to color the sea star and cuts it out. Or, the child may cover the sea star pattern with glue and colored sand to create a rough texture.

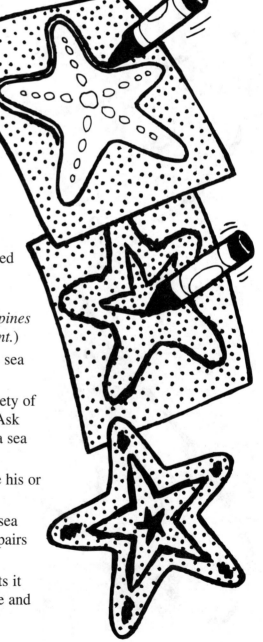

Sea Star Pattern

"Five Little Seashells"

Readiness Standards

Gross Motor
- uses stick puppets to participate in activity

Math
- counts backward
- one-to-one correspondence

Listening
- listens for a variety of purposes
- acts out familiar rhymes

Materials
- Seashell Patterns on page 194 or the color versions, seashell patterns.pdf, on the CD
- "Five Little Seashells" poem (below)
- craft sticks and tape

Teacher Preparation
1. Copy, color, and cut out the Seashell Patterns or make color copies.
2. Using tape, attach each seashell pattern to a craft stick to make a set of seashell stick puppets.

Procedure
1. Say the rhyme "Five Little Seashells" a few times to get the rhythm going.
2. Give each of five children one seashell stick puppet to hold. Have them stand up and hold the puppets so that they are visible to all the children.
3. Encourage the group to help recite the poem as the children with the seashell stick puppets perform the corresponding actions.
4. When each seashell is taken by the waves, a child will sit down with his or her seashell puppet. Continue in this manner until all the seashells have disappeared!
5. Repeat steps 2–4 so that each child has a turn to hold a seashell stick puppet.

"Five Little Seashells"

Five little seashells lying on the shore.
(Five children stand up, each holding up a seashell.)
Swish went the waves, and then there were four.
(One child sits down with seashell.)
Four little seashells cozy as can be.
Swish went the waves, and then there were three.
(One child sits down with seashell.)
Three little seashells all pearly new.
Swish went the waves, and then there were two.
(One child sits down with seashell.)
Two little seashells sleeping in the sun.
Swish went the waves, and then there was one.
(One child sits down with seashell.)
One little seashell left all alone,
Whispered, "Shhhhh," as I took it home.
(The remaining child sits down with a seashell.)

Seashell Patterns

Ocean Shape Toss

Readiness Standards

Social
- takes turns

Gross Motor
- throws beanbag to a target (shape)

Math
- identifies shapes

Materials
- Ocean Shape Patterns on pages 196–197 or the color versions, ocean shapes.pdf, on the CD
- large sheet of bulletin board paper or chart paper
- 3 beanbags
- tape

Teacher Preparation
1. Enlarge and copy, color, and cut out the Ocean Shape Patterns or make color copies.

2. Create an Ocean Shape Toss board. Use tape to attach each ocean shape pattern to the sheet of bulletin board paper or chart paper.

3. Place the Ocean Shape Toss game board on the floor in an easily accessible area of the classroom.

Procedure
1. Gather the children around so that the game board is visible to the whole group.

2. Explain to the children that many ocean animals have shapes similar to the ones they know.

3. Identify which ocean animal is portraying each shape (i.e., sea urchin—circle, cuttlefish—oval, shell—triangle, sea star—star).

4. Explain that you will call out the name of a shape, and one child at a time will try to toss a beanbag on top of that shape.

5. Allow each child to have three chances to hit the object with a bean bag.

6. Continue in this manner until all the children have had a chance to play the game.

7. As skill level (accuracy) improves, encourage the children to stand farther and farther away from the Ocean Shape Toss board.

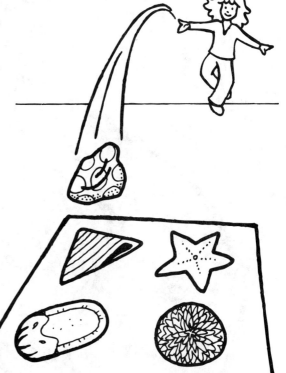

Ocean Shape Patterns

sea urchin

cuttlefish

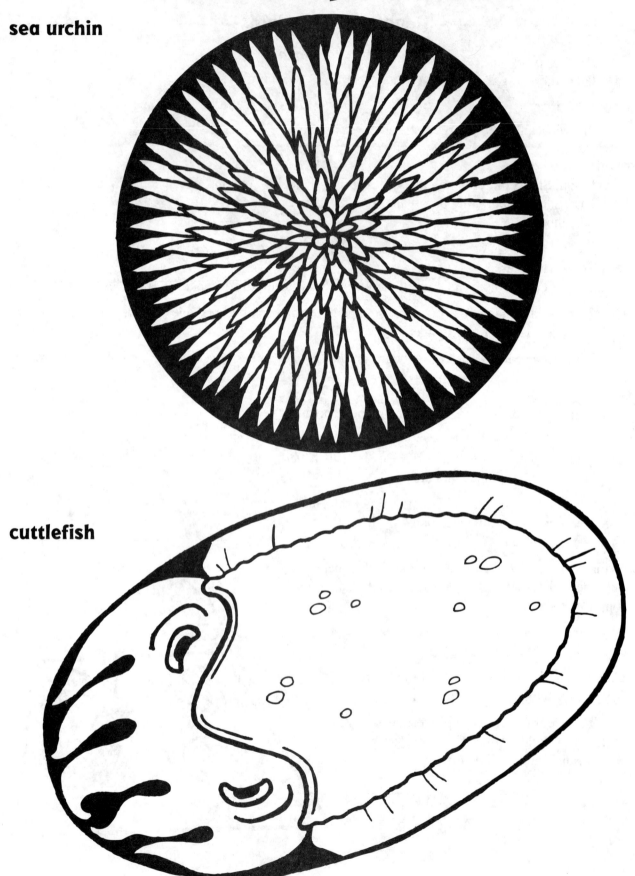

Ocean Shape Patterns (cont.)

seashell

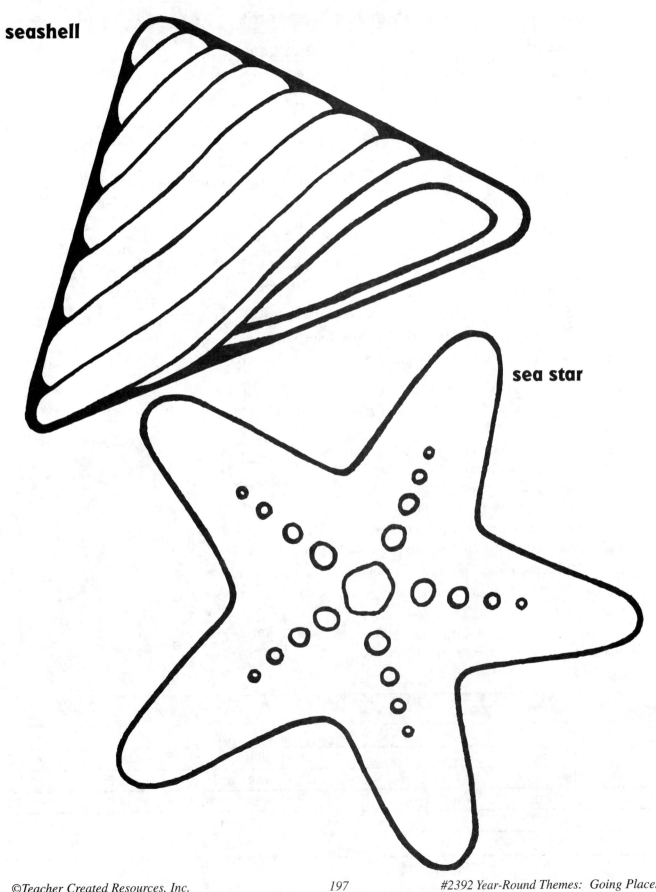

sea star

Ocean Animal Movements

── Readiness Standards ──

Gross Motor
- performs gross-motor movements

Oral Language
- speaks clearly in front of the class

Cognitive
- follows two-step directions

Materials
- Ocean Animal Cards on page 199 or the color versions, ocean animal patterns.pdf, on the CD
- cube-shaped tissue box
- construction paper
- markers
- tape or glue

Teacher Preparation
1. Copy, color, and cut out the Ocean Animal Patterns or make color copies.
2. Use tape to cover the tissue box with construction paper.
3. Tape or glue the six ocean animals on the sides of the tissue box to form a die of ocean animals.

Procedure
1. Explain to the children that they will be playing a game, imitating the movements of several different ocean animals.
2. Show the children each animal on the cube. Talk about the specific movement the children will perform. (See the sample list of movements below.)
3. A child rolls the cube like a die; then he or she uses the picture on the cube to direct the class about which type of ocean animal movement to perform.
4. Each child in the group performs the movement.
5. Another child is selected to roll the cube and repeats steps 3–4.
6. Continue in this manner until each child has had a chance to roll the cube and give directions.

Ocean Animal	Type of Movement
crab	crab walk
dolphin	dive
fish	swim
octopus	wave arms like tentacles
seagull	flap wings to fly
sea anemone	sway back and forth in waves

Ocean Animal Cards

Souvenir Beach Bag

This is the culminating activity for the ocean unit—the take-home souvenir! Assembling this project requires some prep time, depending on the children's cutting abilities. Adult assistance can be helpful and will also provide children with more opportunities to share what they have learned about the ocean while working on the different unit activities. It is suggested that the beach bag be assembled on one day and the Beach medallions on another day.

Beach Bag

Materials

- Souvenir Beach Bag Patterns on page 202 or the color versions, bag patterns.pdf, on the CD

- small paper lunch bags

- markers, glue, and scissors

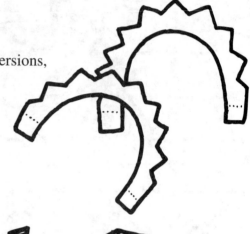

Teacher Preparation

1. Copy twice, cut out, and color the Beach Bag Patterns for each child or make color copies.

2. Cut out the interior semi-circles of the suns. The sun pieces will create the handles for the beach bag.

3. Fold the bag patterns along the dotted lines.

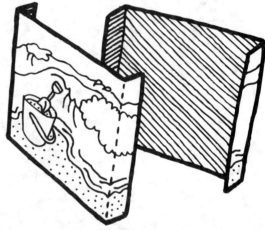

Procedure

1. Glue the bag patterns around the paper bag. Patterns should cover the bottom half of the bag.

2. Cut off the excess bag around the top of the bag patterns.

3. Apply glue to the tab on each sun.

4. Glue one sun handle to the inside top of the front and one to the inside back of the bag.

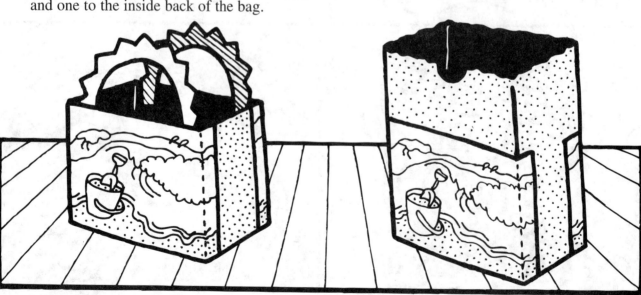

Souvenir Beach Bag *(cont.)*

Beach Medallions

Materials

- Beach Medallion Patterns on pages 203–204 or the color versions, beach medallions.pdf, on the CD
- white cardstock
- yarn or ribbon
- hole punch
- markers

Teacher Preparation

1. Copy the Beach Medallion Patterns onto white cardstock for each child or make color copies.
2. Cut out some or all of the patterns.
3. Cut appropriate lengths of yarn or ribbon for the Beach Medallion necklaces. Be sure to add a little extra for tying the necklaces on to wear.

Procedure

1. Explain to children that they can make a medallion necklace with the patterns they have colored. Color each pattern, if not using the color version.
2. Punch a hole in each pattern where indicated, using a hole punch. Help the children as needed.
3. String the medallions on a length of yarn.
4. Tie the necklace around the child's neck and cut off the remaining yarn.

Souvenir Beach Bag Assembly

Materials

- School-Home Connection Ticket on page 204
- Beach Bag
- Medallions Necklace
- stapler

Teacher Preparation

1. Copy the School-Home Connection Ticket for each child.
2. Collect the beach bags, medallions, and tickets.

Procedure

1. Place the medallion necklace inside the beach bag.
2. Bring the sun handles together and staple the School-Home Connection Ticket between them.
3. Have children take home the Beach Bag Souvenir and necklaces to share with family and friends.

School-Home Connection: To the Ocean

Making the Souvener Beach Bag provides each child with a souvenir of the ocean unit to take home to share what he or she has learned. By sending home this handmade souvenir, along with a copy of the School-Home Connection Ticket, each child will be encouraged to discuss what he or she has learned during the unit. Parents can use the prompts on the ticket as a springboard for discussions, songs, stories, and other activities from the ocean unit.

Teacher Note: Don't forget to have an official passport stamping at the end of the ocean journey.

Souvenir Beach Bag Patterns

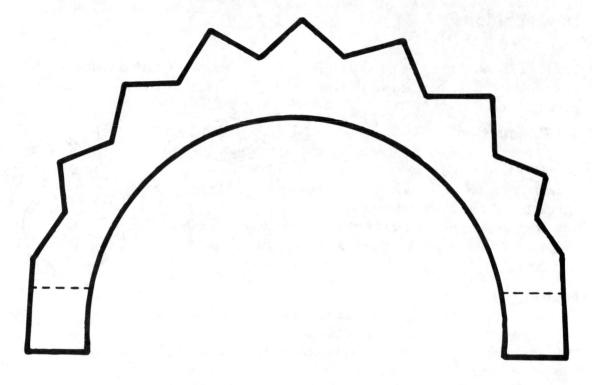

Beach Medallion Patterns

Beach Medallion Patterns *(cont.)*

School-Home Connection Ticket: Ocean

Our class has just finished a study of the ocean. Each day we learned more about ocean life. Look at your child's Souvenir Beach Bag from our "visit" to the ocean. Find out what he or she learned. You might start by discussing the following:

Which ocean animal . . .

— lives only in the water (lives on both the land and in the water)?

— has scales (skin/fins/legs)?

— is a fish (mammal/reptile)?

— swims (crawls/stays still most of the time)?

Which ocean/beach activity . . .

— is your favorite?

— do you collect?

— do you build?

— uses a pole?

Passport

How to Use the Passport Book in Your Travels

After visiting a destination, have the children complete a page in their passport books to document that they have finished the unit. When all the places have been visited, distribute the passport books to the children to take home. Encourage the children to describe the highlights of their visits by sharing the passport books with family and friends.

Passport

Materials

- Passport Patterns on pages 206–208
- storage container for passports
- stamps and stamp pads or stickers
- markers
- stapler
- small photo of each child (optional)

Teacher Preparation

1. Copy and cut out the Passport pages for each child.
2. Assemble a passport for each child.
3. Create a storage area for the passports. They will be stamped after each unit and stored until the next unit is finished. At the end of the year, the completed passports can be taken home.

Procedure

1. At the beginning of the year (or first unit), have each child fill out the title page for his or her passport. Help the child write his or her name and age if necessary.

2. Have each child attach a small photo of him or herself in the rectangle on the title page of the passport. If photos are not available, ask each child to draw a self-portrait and place it in the rectangle provided on the cover of the passport.

3. Have each child color the passport logo on the title page. Assign a student to collect the passports.

4. After finishing each unit, hand out the passports or have a few children hand them out.

5. Have children color the scenes for the unit and place an appropriate stamp or sticker in the box to signify completion of the unit.

6. Assign a passport collector and return the passport book pages for storage after each unit.

7. When all the units have been completed, allow the children to take their assembled passports home to share with their family and friends.

Passport Patterns

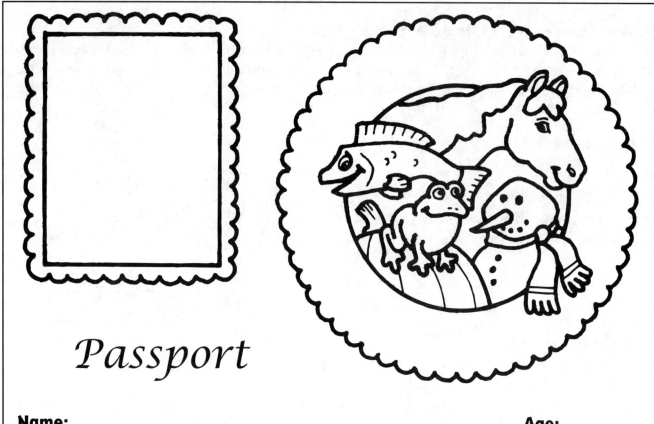

Passport

Name: _____ **Age:** _____

Farm

Passport Patterns *(cont.)*

Pumpkin Patch

Winter Wonderland

Passport Patterns *(cont.)*

Pond

Ocean